TEST-SPECIFIC THINKING

TEACHING STUDENTS to THINK the WAY TESTS MAKE THEM

ROBERT J. MARZANO

BRIDGET CAHILL

JENI GOTTO

BRIAN J. KOSENA

MICHAEL J. LYNCH

LUCY PEARSON

CINDY DAVIS

LINDSAY GRAHAM

BRENDA MARTIN

CLAUDETTE TRUJILLO

Copyright © 2025 by Marzano Resources

Materials appearing here are copyrighted. With one exception, all rights are reserved. Readers may reproduce only those pages marked "Reproducible." Otherwise, no part of this book may be reproduced or transmitted in any form or by any means (electronic, photocopying, recording, or otherwise) without prior written permission of the publisher and the authors. This book, in whole or in part, may not be included in a large language model, used to train AI, or uploaded into any AI system.

AI outputs featured in the text were generated with the assistance of ChatGPT.

555 North Morton Street
Bloomington, IN 47404
800.733.6786 (toll free) / 812.336.7700
FAX: 812.336.7790

email: info@MarzanoResources.com
MarzanoResources.com

Visit **MarzanoResources.com/reproducibles** to download the free reproducibles in this book.

Printed in the United States of America

Library of Congress Cataloging-in-Publication Data

Names: Marzano, Robert J., author.
Title: Test-specific thinking : teaching students to think the way tests make them / Robert J. Marzano, Bridget Cahill, Jeni Gotto, Brian J. Kosena, Michael J. Lynch, Lucy Pearson with Cindy Davis, Lindsay Graham, Brenda Martin, Claudette Trujillo.
Description: Bloomington, IN : Marzano Resources, [2025] | Includes bibliographical references and index.
Identifiers: LCCN 2025001117 (print) | LCCN 2025001118 (ebook) | ISBN 9781943360949 (paperback) | ISBN 9781943360956 (ebook)
Subjects: LCSH: Educational tests and measurements--Evaluation. | Educational tests and measurements--Design and construction. | Academic achievement. | Motivation in education.
Classification: LCC LB3051 .M38 2025 (print) | LCC LB3051 (ebook) | DDC 371.26/1--dc23/eng/20250213
LC record available at https://lccn.loc.gov/2025001117
LC ebook record available at https://lccn.loc.gov/2025001118

Production Team

President and Publisher: Douglas M. Rife
Associate Publishers: Todd Brakke and Kendra Slayton
Editorial Director: Laurel Hecker
Art Director: Rian Anderson
Copy Chief: Jessi Finn
Developmental Editor: Laurel Hecker
Copy Editor: Anne Marie Watkins
Proofreader: Elijah Oates
Text and Cover Designer: Abigail Bowen
Acquisitions Editors: Carol Collins and Hilary Goff
Content Development Specialist: Amy Rubenstein
Associate Editors: Sarah Ludwig and Elijah Oates
Editorial Assistant: Madison Chartier

ACKNOWLEDGMENTS

To the students—watching you embrace the opportunity to think of and create your own item frames has been a joy. Your teachers light up when they talk about your progress and the breakthroughs you've made both individually and collectively.

To the teachers—your continuous embrace of change and opportunities to improve personally and professionally continues to inspire. Thank you for pushing through the adaptation and opportunity that item frames present to your body of work.

To the principals and school leaders—bravo! Systemically folding in item frames and cumulative learning into your deliberate approach to high reliability practices has helped set a new standard for all of us to work toward.

All of you are a beacon for others to embrace research-based practices and authentically define collective efficacy in a personalized competency-based system.

The authors would like to thank Brandon Peterson, Maša Fritz, Elizabeth Gallegos, Chris Tidd, Abigail Anderson, and Grace Mussman for their contributions to the book.

Visit **MarzanoResources.com/reproducibles**
to download the free reproducibles in this book.

TABLE OF CONTENTS

ABOUT THE AUTHORS ix

ABOUT THE CONTRIBUTORS xiii

INTRODUCTION
REVEALING AN INCONVENIENT TRUTH 1

CHAPTER 1
UNDERSTANDING TEST-SPECIFIC THINKING 3
    Test-Specific Thinking 3
    The Rise of Multiple Choice 9
    A Defense of Test-Specific Thinking 11
    The Necessity of Understanding Item Schemas 12
    Summary 15

CHAPTER 2
CONNECTING ELA ITEM FRAMES TO ACADEMIC CONTENT. 17
    Matching Item Frames to Standards 20
    Matching Item Frames to the Curriculum 22
    Matching Item Frames to Common Assessments 23
    Matching Item Frames to Proficiency Scales 25
    Integrating Item Frames Into Proficiency Scales 27
    Focusing on High-Frequency Item Frames 30
    Summary 32

CHAPTER 3
USING ELA ITEM FRAMES IN CLASSROOM INSTRUCTION 35
Step 1: Teach the Content That Is the Focus of the Item Frame. 35

Step 2: Present Students With Potential Strategies
for Approaching the Item 38

Step 3: Provide Students With Multiple Opportunities to Analyze Items . . 39

Summary 44

CHAPTER 4
CONNECTING MATHEMATICS ITEM FRAMES TO ACADEMIC CONTENT 45
Matching Item Frames to Mathematics Standards 47

Matching Item Frames to the Curriculum 49

Matching Item Frames to Common Assessments. 51

Matching Item Frames to Proficiency Scales 52

Integrating Item Frames Into Proficiency Scales 54

Summary 56

CHAPTER 5
USING MATHEMATICS ITEM FRAMES IN CLASSROOM INSTRUCTION 57
Step 1: Teach the Content That Is the Focus of the Item Frame. 57

Step 2: Present Students With Potential Strategies
for Approaching the Item 60

Step 3: Provide Students With Multiple Opportunities to Analyze Items . . .61

Summary 63

CHAPTER 6
SUPPORTING AND INTEGRATING THE USE OF ITEM FRAMES 65
Cumulative Review. 65

Journaling. 70

Questioning Techniques 74

Guided Discourse. 77

The Successive Relearning Instructional Cycle 88

Adaptations From the Field. 89

Summary 99

CHAPTER 7
LEADING ITEM-FRAME USAGE AT THE SCHOOL AND DISTRICT LEVELS **101**

    Misconceptions About *Teaching to the Test* 101

    The Limitations of External Tests 103

    Interpretation of a Student's Score on a Large-Scale Assessment 112

    Schoolwide Initiatives 113

    Adaptations From the Field 123

    Summary 131

EPILOGUE
PULLING BACK THE CURTAIN **133**

REFERENCES AND RESOURCES **135**

INDEX **139**

ABOUT THE AUTHORS

Robert J. Marzano, PhD, is cofounder and chief academic officer of Marzano Resources in Denver, Colorado. During his fifty years in the field of education, he has worked with educators as a speaker and trainer and has authored more than seventy books and 250 articles on topics such as instruction, assessment, writing and implementing standards, cognition, effective leadership, and school intervention. His books include *The New Art and Science of Teaching, Leaders of Learning, Making Classroom Assessments Reliable and Valid, The Classroom Strategies Series, Managing the Inner World of Teaching, A Handbook for High Reliability Schools, A Handbook for Personalized Competency-Based Education,* and *The Highly Engaged Classroom*. His practical translations of the most current research and theory into classroom strategies are known internationally and are widely practiced by both teachers and administrators.

Dr. Marzano received a bachelor's degree from Iona College in New York, a master's degree from Seattle University, and a doctorate from the University of Washington.

To learn more about Dr. Marzano, visit www.marzanoresources.com.

Bridget Cahill is an ardent advocate for competency-based education, bringing years of expertise in instructional planning, professional development, and fostering learner-centered learning environments. As a dedicated educational leader, she has led districtwide initiatives to enhance instructional practices and empower learners. She supports teachers and administrators to help them transform the philosophy of competency-based education into actionable practices by designing personalized learning experiences that empower students to take ownership of their learning.

Cahill's experiences as an educator began with teaching abroad, and her career in public education began as a middle school science teacher. Before becoming a leader at the district level, she was a middle school teacher in Westminster Public Schools for thirteen years, where she planned and implemented competency-based instruction in science, literacy, and English language development.

Cahill holds a master's degree in educational equity and cultural diversity from the University of Colorado Boulder, along with a master's degree in curriculum and instruction and a bachelor's degree in marine science and biology.

Jeni Gotto, EdD, brings over twenty-five years of transformative leadership to the pages of this book. As superintendent of Westminster Public Schools, Dr. Gotto leads with an unwavering commitment to equity and innovation, ensuring that every student, regardless of background, has the opportunity to succeed. Her pioneering work in competency-based education (CBE) has redefined learning for countless students, blending rigor with personalized pathways to achievement.

From her early days as a vocational teacher in a small rural district to her current role as a U.S. thought leader, Dr. Gotto has dedicated her career to reshaping education. As the superintendent of the largest districtwide implementation of competency-based education for preK–12, she oversees groundbreaking initiatives that set a new standard for personalized and equitable learning. Her efforts in curriculum design, assessment, and high reliability organizational practices have not only improved school systems but also inspired educators worldwide. A compelling speaker and global trainer, she has shared her expertise in forums ranging from U.S. conferences to international symposia, leaving a lasting impact on the future of learning. Her innovative approaches and dedication have earned her prestigious accolades, including the Colorado Association of Leaders in Educational Technology Dan Maas Technology Leadership Award and multiple grants to advance educational practice.

Dr. Gotto holds a doctor of education in leadership for educational equity from the University of Colorado Denver, along with a master's degree in administrative leadership and policy studies.

About the Authors

Brian J. Kosena, EdD, serves as the chief learning officer for Westminster Public Schools in Westminster, Colorado. Previously, he was the founding principal of John E. Flynn A Marzano Academy, a preK–8 school of innovation within Westminster Public Schools.

An educator since 2006, Dr. Kosena has served as a principal, instructional technology coordinator, and high school social studies teacher. His experience ranges from teaching in a private Jesuit high school to leading a predominantly low-income public elementary school. Additionally, he has taught graduate-level and teacher-licensure courses in the Denver metropolitan area, sharing his knowledge of and passion for innovative education practices.

Dr. Kosena is a coauthor of several books, including *Leading a Competency-Based Elementary School* and *Pioneers of Personalized Education: Westminster Public Schools and the Pursuit of Competency-Based Learning*. These works reflect his expertise in competency-based education (CBE) and his commitment to transforming educational systems to meet the needs of all learners.

A strong advocate for CBE, Dr. Kosena works in Westminster Public Schools, a leader in CBE innovation and design in the United States. He conducts formal research on CBE instructional practices, regularly presents at conferences, and provides practical, scalable solutions for overcoming challenges in CBE implementation.

Dr. Kosena earned a bachelor's degree in international affairs from the University of Colorado Boulder, a master's degree in secondary education from the University of Phoenix, and a doctorate in leadership for educational equity from the University of Colorado Denver.

Michael J. Lynch is a distinguished educational leader with over thirty years of experience as a teacher, coach, principal, academic director, and executive. He has dedicated his career to empowering school leaders across diverse communities in multiple school districts in Colorado. A lead trainer for McREL's Balanced Leadership program, he has facilitated professional development for districts of all sizes and served as a graduate-level instructor for several esteemed colleges and universities.

Lynch specializes in fostering collaboration among principals, new teachers, and mentors, with a particular focus on competency-based education and High Reliability Schools. His expertise spans from spearheading school-improvement initiatives in turnaround schools to cultivating excellence in high-performing school communities.

An accomplished speaker and trainer in the United States, Lynch is known for his ability to galvanize school and district teams, driving initiatives that result in meaningful and lasting impact.

Lynch holds a bachelor's degree in sociology and human services from Fort Lewis College and a secondary education degree from Metropolitan State University of Denver. He also received a master's degree in education administration and supervision from the University of Phoenix and has completed the administrator/superintendent license program from the University of Colorado Colorado Springs.

Lucy Pearson, assistant principal at John E. Flynn A Marzano Academy, brings over a decade of experience in various educational roles within Westminster Public Schools. Her background includes teaching across different grade levels, specializing in kindergarten and level 3–4, and serving as a special education interventionist and instructional coach. Pearson's commitment to building strong relationships with students and families, combined with her innovative teaching approach, enhances the educational experience at John E. Flynn.

Beyond her professional life, Pearson enjoys outdoor adventures with her dog, shares a passion for soccer, and embraces challenges such as completing a marathon in Dublin, Ireland. With academic credentials from Queen's University, University of Colorado Denver, and Regis University, Pearson's dedication to learning and growth contributes to her role as a vital member of the school community, shaping a bright future with energy and determination.

TO BOOK BRIAN J. KOSENA OR MICHAEL J. LYNCH
FOR PROFESSIONAL DEVELOPMENT,
CONTACT PD@MARZANORESOURCES.COM.

ABOUT THE CONTRIBUTORS

Cindy Davis is principal of Sherrelwood Elementary, a competency-based PK–5 elementary school. She has been in Westminster Public Schools for forty years, beginning as a paraprofessional, then serving as a Title I teacher for twelve years, a literacy coordinator for twelve years, and now at her current school as principal for sixteen years.

Davis spent much of her career as a literacy specialist and providing professional development across the district in many capacities. One of her favorite areas was competency-based education. Before beginning her work at Sherrelwood Elementary, she spent over a year leading a team and developing competencies at all levels in literacy. She has spent her time mentoring other principals and finds it rewarding to support other principals through a similar endeavor in their schools.

With her staff, she loves developing leadership and building capacities so the school has ownership by all staff members, especially with competency-based systems. Many other schools and organizations have come to visit the school to learn about competency-based education in action, from the early years of development to a more sophisticated level.

Davis has attended or presented at several competency-based conferences, such as iNACOL, Aurora Institute, Marzano HRS Conference, CASE, and her own district's Competency-Based Education Summit. She has learned a lot to apply at her own school, and this is what she hopes to do for others. Davis and her school now hold Marzano High Reliability School Level 5 status and continue to be proud of their accomplishments.

Davis received a bachelor's degree in education from Illinois State University and a master's in educational leadership from the University of Phoenix.

Lindsay Graham is a writer and developer with Marzano Academies. She has over ten years of experience in competency-based education and working with schools transitioning to CBE.

Graham received a bachelor's degree from the University of Colorado and a master's degree from the University of Iowa's Writers' Workshop.

Brenda Martin is the current director of schools for Westminster Public Schools, bringing over two decades of experience in education. She served as a principal and school administrator for eleven years and previously worked as a teacher and instructional coach for another thirteen years. Martin holds a master's degree in curriculum and development and is deeply passionate about empowering educators through meaningful training and support. She believes that strong leadership and well-equipped teachers are key to student success. Outside of work, Martin is a proud wife and mother of two, balancing her professional commitment with the joys of family life.

Claudette Trujillo is a visionary leader, poet, published contributing author, and comedian. She is the principal of Metropolitan Arts Academy in Westminster, Colorado. With twenty-five years in education, she has served in various roles, including teacher, instructional coach, and administration, gaining experience in levels PK–12. For the past sixteen years, she has focused on competency-based systems, advocating for equity, innovation, and personalized learning.

Under her leadership, Metropolitan Arts Academy became the second school in the nation to earn Level 5 High Reliability School Certification through Marzano Resources. She currently serves as co-chair of the Council for Equity and Educational Opportunities in Westminster Public Schools. Trujillo has contributed to national discussions on competency-based education, attending and presenting at conferences such as the National Summit on Competency-Based Education and the Aurora Symposium. She has also facilitated CBE professional development with the Re-Inventing Schools Coalition in Maine.

A published contributing author, Trujillo's work has appeared in publications by the Aurora Institute and Competency Works. Her leadership and insights have been featured in interviews, including Getting Smart and the entrustED, podcasts for educators. She proudly served as a keynote panelist at the esteemed Aurora Symposium in 2023.

Trujillo holds a deep connection to her school community, not only as an alumna of Westminster Public Schools but also as a parent and grandparent of students in the competency-based model.

Trujillo earned her bachelor of arts in secondary English with a minor in special education from Metropolitan State University of Denver and her master of education in educational counseling and principal license from University of Phoenix.

INTRODUCTION
REVEALING AN INCONVENIENT TRUTH

Every year, millions of U.S. students take a variety of tests developed by organizations and companies other than their classroom teachers. For example, end-of-year external tests are mandated or strongly encouraged in every state. Additionally, many districts across the country employ interim assessments multiple times during the school year that are intended to measure students' academic growth and forecast how well they will do on the end-of-year tests. If students' scores on interim assessments indicate that they might do poorly on the end-of-year test, then teachers make extra efforts to mitigate the projected underperformance.

It's safe to say that external tests (that is, those designed outside of the confines of the school) are a regular part of students' lives, and their use continues beyond end-of-year tests. In fact, many students will have to take a variety of types of assessments throughout their lives. Students going to college will take the SAT or the ACT. Students going on to graduate school will take the GREs. Students going to law school will take the LSAT. Those going on to be mechanics will take one or more of the Automotive Service Excellence tests. Those going into plumbing will take a plumbing aptitude exam, and so on.

At first blush, all this testing and interpretation of test scores seems not only logical but necessary. Isn't it obvious that students should be tested to determine their competence in various domains? Once these competencies are known, students can be properly guided on their future academic and life choices. One might say that this is the culture of K–12 schooling in the United States, which has a system designed to measure and sort students into categories that guide them to their correct life paths. But this idyllic scenario falls apart quickly when one examines the assumptions underlying this process.

More pointedly, the assumption that a student's score on a specific test is a highly accurate indicator of their expertise is simply not accurate. This book will demonstrate this problem in great detail and, more importantly, disclose the fact that the very structure of the items themselves and the directions examinees are required to follow when taking the test represent a type of thinking that goes well beyond the content being tested. We refer to this type of thinking as *test-specific thinking*. Herein lies the major source of error in students' scores: They might know the content but not be cognizant of the test-specific thinking required to demonstrate their knowledge. Herein also lies the remedy for this problem: Make sure students are well versed in the requisite test-specific thinking as well as the academic content.

The fundamental tenet of this book is that the structures and particularities of assessment items that aren't directly related to the content the item is designed to test should be directly taught to students along with the content that is the focus of items. The chapters in this book are designed to provide the information and protocols to do so. Chapter 1 introduces the concept of test-specific thinking and delves into why it is so essential that students learn how test questions are constructed. Chapter 2 (page 17) deals with understanding item schemas in the English language arts (ELA), and chapter 3 (page 35) addresses how to use these schemas in the classroom. Chapter 4 (page 45) deals with understanding item schemas in mathematics, and chapter 5 (page 57) addresses how to use these schemas in the classroom. Chapter 6 (page 65) describes various processes and protocols that can be used to support and integrate item schemas in the classroom. Last, chapter 7 (page 101) addresses the school leader's role in these processes.

While this book focuses on the content areas of mathematics and ELA, the basics of teaching item-specific thinking apply to any content area that employs traditional testing methods. This book presents not only classroom approaches but also specific strategies for school leaders to introduce the concept of test-specific thinking to their faculties as part of a schoolwide or districtwide initiative. In effect, this book is useful for K–12 teachers as well as school and district administrators.

Finally, it is important to note that this book was developed over the course of four years. All the strategies and techniques that students should know to engage in effective test-specific thinking have been employed and vetted by K–12 classroom teachers. You will hear their voices and be party to their experiences throughout the text. You will also hear from students and school leaders. Let's begin.

CHAPTER 1

UNDERSTANDING TEST-SPECIFIC THINKING

This chapter begins to explain the shortcomings of external tests by defining test-specific thinking, considering how the format of external test items (in particular, multiple-choice questions) presents an obstacle to students' demonstrating their knowledge, and making the case for explicitly teaching students how test items are constructed.

TEST-SPECIFIC THINKING

One of the more disturbing aspects of external assessments that has come to the attention of educators is that the items on these tests require types of thinking that go above and beyond the type of thinking inherent in the academic content they are designed to measure. We refer to this type of thinking as *test-specific thinking*.

To illustrate, consider the fourth-grade reading test item in figure 1.1 (page 4). On the surface, it appears that the purpose of this item is to determine the ability of fourth-grade students to read a passage and then identify its main idea. Indeed, this purpose is made explicit in the question in part A: "What is the main idea of the text?" In the world outside the classroom, this skill might manifest as a student reading a passage on the internet and then determining the basic message from that text. Similarly, a student might read a chapter in a story and determine how the events in this new chapter add to the basic plot of the story thus far. Certainly, this is an important skill for students to develop. It is also important that educators systematically assess students on this skill to ascertain their status and growth.

But the question that is the centerpiece of this book is, Does this particular item (and others like it on external assessments) truly measure that skill of determining the main idea in a pure and unadorned manner as experienced in the day-to-day world?

Cicadas: Misunderstood Marvels

Every seventeen years, millions of insects emerge from the ground at the same time. Even if you don't see them, you will hear them. All these bugs buzzing at once can make a roaring sound. These noisy critters are called *cicadas*. People used to think of cicadas as pests or plagues, but there's no reason to be afraid of these fascinating creatures.

A Strange Life Cycle

Cicadas have an unusual life cycle. After hatching from eggs above ground, young cicadas dig underneath trees. The young bugs are called *nymphs*. They suck sap from the trees' roots. They stay there for the next two to seventeen years. The bugs that come out every seventeen years are called *periodical cicadas*. After they come up from the ground, cicadas shed their skin. Then they mate and lay eggs. The loud buzzing is the sound of males singing to attract mates. Cicadas only live for about five weeks above ground. The new eggs hatch, and the life cycle begins again.

Their Bark Is Worse Than Their Bite

Before scientists learned more about cicadas, many people thought they were dangerous. The Pilgrims saw a swarm of them in 1633. They had never seen cicadas before. One of their leaders wrote that the bugs "ate green things, and made such a constant yelling noise as made all the woods ring of them . . . ready to deafen the hearers." He also thought the bugs made people sick. Other people thought they destroyed crops. For years, cicadas had a bad reputation.

In fact, scientists have found that cicadas do not hurt crops or plants. They also do not sting or bite people. They are harmless, except for the loud noise they make.

More to Discover

Scientists are still trying to find out more about cicadas. For example, they want to know why some of them stay underground for a certain number of years. They also want to learn how cicadas know to come out of the ground all at the same time. Some cicadas have come out ahead of schedule. Researchers want to know why that happened.

Other scientists have discovered things about cicadas that could help people. Cicadas' wings can clean themselves. Their wings can also keep water off and kill germs. Studying these wings might help engineers make materials that can do the same things. The more we learn about cicadas, the more we can see they are super interesting, not scary!

Part A

What is the main idea of the text?
   a. Cicadas are very useful animals.
   b. Scientists know very little about cicadas.
   c. People in the past were not as smart as people are today.
   d. Cicadas are interesting, not frightening.

Part B

What evidence best supports the answer to part A?
   a. Then they mate and lay eggs.
   b. They had never seen cicadas before.
   c. In fact, scientists have found that cicadas do not hurt crops or plants.
   d. Some cicadas have come out ahead of schedule.

Source for passage: Bradford, 1898; Levy, 2020; Shaw, n.d.

FIGURE 1.1: Fourth-grade reading item.

The answer to this question is an unequivocal *no*. In fact, this item adds much to the basic process of reading for the main idea. To illustrate, consider the two parts to this item. Part A appears to address the ability to read a passage and determine the overall main idea conveyed by the text. A pure measure of this skill would be for students to read the text and then describe the overall meaning of the text orally or in writing. The very act of providing a series of already-articulated main ideas and then asking students to select the "correct" main idea adds significant test-specific thinking to the task.

Obviously, this scenario never occurs outside of school. Readers wishing to discern the main idea of what they are reading might take some time to outline what they have read in their mind in an attempt to capture the overall message of the passage. That overall message has historically been referred to as the *gist* of the information (Kintsch, 1974). The gist of the information one reads is constructed by the person doing the reading; the gist of a passage might be thought of as the reader's attempt to create a summary statement of the main idea. This natural process is certainly an aspect of what students have to do when answering this item. But these summary statements can be quite different from reader to reader. For example, the following are main-idea summary statements for the passage in figure 1.1 generated independently by three adult readers.

- *"Cicadas have a very complex life cycle and society that is of interest to scientists."*
- *"Cicadas were originally thought to be dangerous bugs, but now are studied to determine how they live and prosper."*
- *"The life cycle of cicadas can provide scientists with useful information."*

Unlike constructing the gist when reading in a natural context, when an item like the one in figure 1.1 is involved, students must contrast their conceptions of the main idea of the passage with the options presented to them. Sometimes there is a mismatch between the gist generated by the reader and the main idea statements provided in the item. For example, consider the alternatives the item offers for the main idea.

a. Cicadas are very useful animals.
b. Scientists know very little about cicadas.
c. People in the past were not as smart as people are today.
d. Cicadas are interesting, not frightening.

To answer this item correctly, the reader must contrast their main idea statement with those provided. In this case, none of the options provide a direct match with any of the three statements generated by adult readers. Exacerbating the issue, three of the four options provided in the item contain inaccurate information: Option A states the cicadas are very useful animals; there is nothing in the passage that directly supports this. Option B states that scientists know very little about cicadas. While the passage states that scientists are still studying cicadas, the passage also states that scientists actually know quite a bit about them. Option C states that people in the past were not as smart as people are today. While it is true that the passage begins with a description of how inaccurate the early settlers were about cicadas, this was only a small part of the passage. Additionally, the passage does not directly state anything about the presumed intelligence of the early settlers. The only option that contains accurate summary information about the passage is option D. Thus, answering this item correctly is more a process of ruling out illogical possibilities than it is about generating a main idea statement. This is an added type of thinking that only occurs in test items—hence the term *test-specific thinking*.

In part B of the item in figure 1.1 (page 4), the test-specific thinking becomes even more apparent. Notice that part B of this item asks students, "What evidence best supports the answer to part A?" Obviously, the assumption underlying part B of the item is that the student goes back to the text and finds specific phrases and sentences that support the correct answer. However, as indicated in the previous discussion, it is unlikely that a reader will construct a main idea statement that is precisely the same as the correct response for part A. In effect, part B requires the examinee to find textual evidence for a main idea statement that was not of their own design. This is clearly another aspect of test-specific thinking.

Finally, the act of going back to the text to find evidence for one's conclusions is not something that readers typically do in everyday reading activities. Certainly, readers use information from the text to form conclusions about the main idea, but they rarely, if ever, mark that textual evidence as proof of their conclusions.

This same type of test-specific thinking occurs in many mathematics test items. Consider the example of a third-grade item in figure 1.2. This item pertains to the skill of reading bar graphs. In day-to-day life, people are certainly sometimes required to read and understand bar graphs to gather information. This typically involves understanding the scale of the bar graph and the categories of elements depicted in the bars. In figure 1.2, the scale represents frequency of items and ranges from 0 to 8. The categories of elements are types of animals at the zoo: zebras, giraffes, hippos, elephants, and gazelles. Once a reader knows the scale and the categories, they can construct a general understanding of the information in the bar graph. In this case, that general understanding would be that the zoo has more giraffes (six) and fewer hippos (one) than any other animal. In between are zebras, elephants, and gazelles, which have two or three members of their species represented at the zoo.

In contrast to this typical approach to reading a bar graph, the test item asks the test taker to make calculations they probably wouldn't make when reading a bar

> There are 15 animals in a zoo exhibit. There are 5 different types of animals. The bar graph shows the number of each type of animal.
>
> **Part A**
> How many more giraffes are there than zebras?
> Fill in your answer in the box.
>
> **Part B**
> What is the difference between the number of hippos and the number of giraffes and zebras combined?
> Fill in your answer in the box.
>
>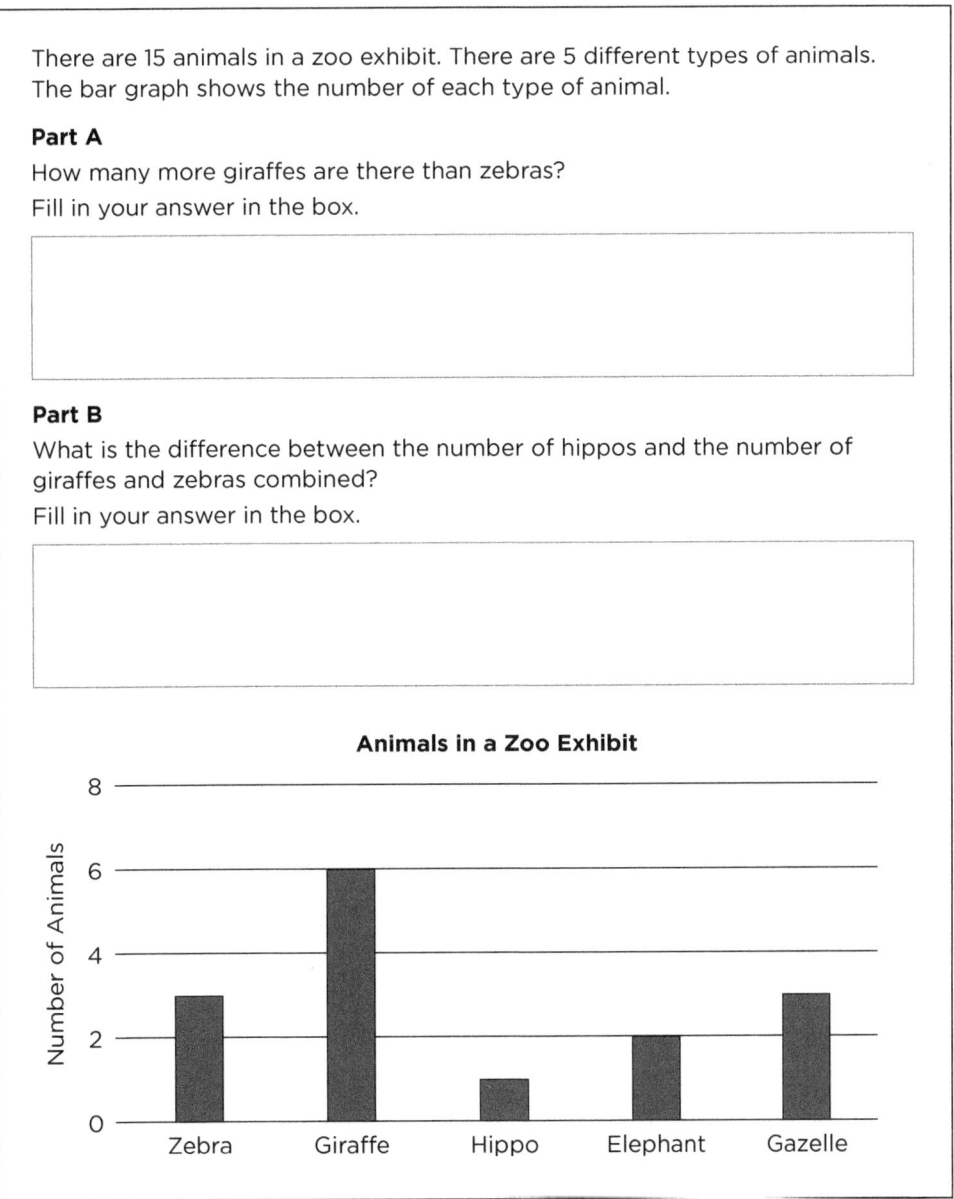

FIGURE 1.2: Third-grade mathematics item.

graph. For example, the test taker must determine the difference between the number of hippos and the number of zebras and giraffes combined. Admittedly, these are simple calculations. There is only one hippo. There are three zebras and six giraffes, for a total of nine animals in the two categories. So, the difference between the number of hippos and the number of zebras and giraffes combined is eight.

But this is not a typical set of calculations one would naturally perform when reading a bar graph. Why would a reader combine categories and then contrast those combined categories with other categories in the graph? Additionally, these calculations have more to do with the ability to add and subtract than they do with the ability to read a bar graph. This is another more subtle example of test-specific thinking. While the basic skill of reading a bar graph is certainly a part of this item, it still requires the test taker to engage in thinking not commonly associated with that skill.

What is clear from these examples is that, to answer items on many of the mandatory large-scale tests in the various academic subject areas, students must execute test-specific types of thinking, some of which have little to do with the academic content being tested. Consequently, students might know the academic content being tested but answer items incorrectly because they are not familiar with the required test-specific thinking. To illustrate, let's go back to the reading item in figure 1.1 (page 4). Imagine that a particular student understands the main idea of the passage about cicadas and therefore gets part A of the item correct. However, the student is not familiar with the idea of identifying a specific part of the passage that discloses the main idea. Consequently, the student answers part B of the item incorrectly. However, another student who is more familiar and comfortable with this convention answers part B correctly because of this background knowledge and comfort level. The same thing might occur with the mathematics item focused on the bar graph. A student might understand the nature of bar graphs and how to read them but not be accustomed to performing the additional calculations that are embedded in answering the items and their various parts.

Test-specific thinking is not a new discovery in the world of testing and measurement. Indeed, it is a central aspect of what measurement experts refer to as *construct-irrelevant variance*. This is the technical term for those characteristics of a test or items on a test that have little or nothing to do with the content but can cause a test taker to incorrectly answer an item, even though the test taker knows the content that is the focus of the item. We discuss the technical aspects of construct-irrelevant variance in chapter 7 (page 101). Here, we simply note that this is the very phenomenon we have demonstrated in the previous section. Test designers have been aware of this phenomenon since at least the late 1980s. Samuel Messick (1989), a validity theorist, described test-specific thinking that causes construct-irrelevant variance this way: "Tests are imperfect measures of constructs because they either leave out something that should be included . . . or else include something that should be left out, or both" (p. 34). In chapter 7 (page 101), we address the various facets of construct-irrelevant variance in some depth. The majority of this book focuses specifically on how individual test items contribute to construct-irrelevant variance.

As you progress through this book, you will note that the multiple-choice format of many items contributes significantly to construct-irrelevant variance. In fact, one can argue that the multiple-choice format in itself detracts from the ability to validly measure students' knowledge and skill relative to specific academic topics. A reasonable question at this juncture is, Where did the concept of a multiple-choice test item come from?

THE RISE OF MULTIPLE CHOICE

The practice of testing has been around for centuries. In fact, formal testing in China can be traced back to the 6th century. According to the U.S. Congress, Office of Technology Assessment (1992):

> The first examinations were attributed to the Sui emperors (589–618 A.D.) in China. With its flexible writing system and extensive body of recorded knowledge, China was in a position much earlier than the West to develop written examinations. The examinations were built around candidates' ability to memorize, comprehend, and interpret classical texts. Aspirants prepared for the examinations on their own in private schools run by scholars or through private tutorials. Some took examinations as early as age 15, while others continued their studies into their thirties. After passing a regional examination, successful applicants traveled to the capital city to take a 3-day examination, with answers evaluated by a special examining board appointed by the Emperor. (p. 148)

In contrast to the long history of formal testing in general, the multiple-choice item appeared relatively recently. The first use of multiple-choice test items is typically attributed to Frederick James Kelly in 1916, and "since then, multiple choice has become the dominant format of standardized achievement tests" (U.S. Congress, Office of Technology Assessment, 1992, p. 117).

Kelly's motivation for developing the multiple-choice format came from studies he analyzed and studies he conducted on how teachers in U.S. schools "assigned marks." He published his findings in the book *Teachers' Marks: Their Variability and Standardization* (Kelly, 1914). Kelly came to a number of conclusions as a consequence of his research, but perhaps his seminal finding was that teachers, even when given the same set of criteria or student work, often award significantly different marks to students. This inconsistency can arise from a number of factors, including differences in interpretation of the grading standards, personal biases, or varying levels of leniency or strictness. Kelly highlighted the influence of subjective factors in grading—such as a teacher's expectations, attitudes toward the student, and personal experiences—as a major cause for variability in marking. To address this variability, Kelly advocated for clearer and more standardized grading criteria. He reasoned that, by doing so, the education system could reduce inconsistencies and make grades more reliable measures of student performance.

Given these conclusions, Kelly set out to design a test that met these criteria. That test was the Kansas Silent Reading Test (Kelly, 1916). In discussing the design of a test like this, Kelly (1916) noted that to be valid, a test:

> should be so simple in its arrangement and in the plan for giving it and scoring the results derived from it that a teacher unskilled in the use of standard tests can understand without difficulty what is expected of her in giving and scoring the test. (p. 63)

Kelly argued that using a standardized test like the Kansas Silent Reading Test allows teachers to reduce subjective judgment when evaluating reading skills and rely on more objective, comparable data to assess students' abilities. Figure 1.3 contains a sample of the directions to teachers Kelly used in his test along with a sample item.

Directions for Giving the Tests
After telling the children not to open the papers, ask the children on the front seats to distribute the papers, placing one upon the desk of each pupil in the class. Have each child fill in the blank space at the top of this page. Then make clear the following:

Instruction to be Read by Teacher and Pupils Together:
This little five-minute game is given to see how quickly and accurately pupils can read silently. To show what sort of game it is, let us read this:
Below are given the names of four animals. Draw a line around the name of each animal that is useful on the farm:

        cow   tiger   rat   wolf

This exercise tells us to draw a line around the word, cow. No other answer is right. Even if a line is drawn under the word cow, the exercise is wrong, and counts nothing. The game consists of a lot of just such exercises, so it is wise to study each exercise carefully enough to be sure that you know exactly what you are asked to do. The number of exercises which you can finish in five minutes will make your score, so do them as fast as you can, being sure to do them right. Stop at once when time is called. Do not open the papers until told, so that all may begin at the same time.

The teacher should then be sure that each pupil has a good pencil or pen. Note the minute and second by the watch, and say, begin.
Allow exactly five minutes.
Answer no questions of the pupils which arise from not understanding what to do with any given exercise. When time is up say stop and then collect the papers at once.

Source: Kelly, 1916, p. 65.
FIGURE 1.3: Sample from Kelly's silent reading test.

The use of multiple-choice items probably appeared rather inconsequential at the time of their introduction. Who could have predicted that they would become the predominant vehicles of determining examinees' knowledge and skill across the planet in almost every academic domain and across all age levels?

World War I ignited the most rapid expansion of school testing and the use of multiple-choice items. In 1917, the U.S. Army recruited scholars from the American Psychological Association to develop group intelligence tests, which later became the Alpha and Beta tests. The Alpha test, in particular, measured test takers' verbal aptitude and made extensive use of multiple-choice items. The army used this test to quickly determine which recruits were capable of service and assign them to specific jobs (U.S. Congress, Office of Technology Assessment, 1992). From that point on, multiple-choice items and their derivatives were the staple of educational testing.

Over time, they quite naturally made their way into the classroom. Teachers were taught to use them as they designed their own quizzes and tests. Teacher teams used them to develop common assessments, companies used them to develop interim assessments, and states used them in their end-of-year assessments. They became ubiquitous.

A DEFENSE OF TEST-SPECIFIC THINKING

Thus far, we might have given the impression that we are critical of test-specific thinking. It is certainly true that we believe ignoring the specific types of thinking tests require can result in scores that are highly inaccurate—and even invalid—for many students. But this source of error can be mitigated; this book presents suggestions educators can use to that end. Additionally, much of what we refer to as *test-specific thinking* involves mental processes that researchers from a number of academic areas have asserted should be explicitly taught in schools. To illustrate, consider the domain of reading.

Researchers and theorists in the English language arts (ELA) have long called for schools to emphasize close-reading skills. Arguably, one might say that the close-reading movement became prominent in 2006, when ACT released *Reading Between the Lines: What the ACT Reveals About College Readiness in Reading*, a report warning that a significant proportion of high school graduates in the United States were not ready for college-level reading. Specifically, the report stated that only 51 percent of high school graduates were prepared for the types of thinking required in college—the lowest point in more than a decade.

The ACT study went on to explain that the deficiencies in reading skills of U.S. students primarily were found in their inability to read *complex texts*, defined as those involving a great deal of information that is related in integrated and embedded ways. Complex texts also exhibit relationships between multiple characters, unconventional structure, intricate style, context-dependent vocabulary, and abstract literary devices.

The ability to read and comprehend such texts was found to be "the clearest differentiator in reading between students who are likely to be ready for college and those who are not," a relationship that held true across genders, racial and ethnic groups, and family income levels (ACT, 2006, pp. 16–17).

Similar deficiencies were found in students' abilities to address complex mathematical items and science items (Student Achievement Partners, 2018). In mathematics assessments, many of the item-specific types of thinking have been highlighted directly and indirectly in the evolution of the various standards documents for mathematics. For example, in the Common Core mathematics standards (National Governors Association Center for Best Practices & Council of Chief State School Officers [NGA & CCSSO], 2010b), some skills that would qualify as test-specific thinking were specified in the Standards for Mathematical Practice. Similarly, in the Next Generation Science Standards (NGSS Lead States, 2013), some of the more generalizable skills were akin to test-specific thinking. For example, the skill of making sense of problems and persevering in solving them in mathematics, the skill of identifying inconsistencies in data in science, and the skill of evidence-based thinking from both subject-area standards are all similar to many of the test-specific thinking strategies discussed in this book. Finally, many of the test-specific types of thinking we have identified date back to the thinking skills movement in the 1980s as described in the book *Dimensions of Thinking: A Framework for Curriculum and Instruction* (Marzano et al., 1988). From the perspective of this work, one might reasonably conclude that there continue to be movements and mandates in education to directly teach these types of skills in the classroom. In effect, teaching test-specific thinking as defined in this book reinforces a number of general cognitive skills indigenous to various subject-area experts.

THE NECESSITY OF UNDERSTANDING ITEM SCHEMAS

Another way to understand the concept of teaching test-specific thinking is that schools should ensure all students are aware of the schema for any given item in the tests they will be asked to take. *Schemas* (or *schemata*) allow us to make sense of the world around us by providing a framework for understanding and categorizing various aspects of our environment. In terms of human perceptions, a schema can be understood as a mental framework or structure that helps individuals organize and interpret information based on their past experiences, knowledge, beliefs, and expectations. The concept of schema first became popular in the world of education in the 1970s when psychologists like Roger C. Schank and Robert P. Abelson (1977) demonstrated the importance of schema in human cognition. The following are everyday examples of schemas people use.

- **Restaurant schema:** When you enter a restaurant, you have a preconceived schema (or mental framework) about what to expect based on your past experiences. This schema includes expectations about the layout of the restaurant and the presence of tables, chairs, waitstaff, and a menu. Your schema also includes expectations about the process of ordering food, receiving service, and paying the bill.
- **Dog schema:** If you encounter a dog, you draw on your existing schema for dogs based on past experiences or knowledge. Your dog schema might include expectations about the dog's appearance, behavior, and characteristics such as barking, wagging its tail, and being friendly or cautious around strangers.
- **Job interview schema:** Before going to a job interview, you likely have a schema about what to expect based on your understanding of typical interview processes. Your schema includes expectations about dressing professionally, arriving on time, answering questions confidently, and behaving professionally throughout the interview.
- **Supermarket schema:** When you enter a supermarket, you rely on your supermarket schema to navigate the store efficiently. This schema includes expectations about the layout of different sections, such as produce, dairy, and canned goods. Your schema also helps you anticipate where to find specific items based on your previous experiences or the typical organization of similar supermarkets.
- **Traffic light schema:** As you approach a traffic light while driving, you rely on your schema for traffic lights to interpret the signals correctly. Your schema includes expectations about the meaning of different colored lights (red, yellow, green) and their corresponding actions (stop, slow down, go) based on traffic laws and previous driving experiences.

Without a schema for a particular situation, that situation will be uninterpretable to an individual, even though that individual might recognize some of the parts. The following paragraph from the book *Ethical Test Preparation in the Classroom* (Marzano, Dodson, Simms, & Wipf, 2022) illustrates the importance of schemata when reading text:

> If the cord around the milk loosened it could drop, perhaps injuring pedestrians. A break in the clothesline would likewise cause a fall. Alternatively, a jam in either pulley would leave the milk stuck in the middle or high winds could cause it to sway and possibly spill. It is clear that the best solution would involve ground travel, in which the least number of things could go wrong. (p. 169)

Most likely, you have little idea what this passage is about, even though you recognize every word in the paragraph and even comprehend the meaning of specific clauses and phrases. The reason comprehension of the passage eludes you at this particular moment is that you have no schema or mental model for what the passage is referring to. The picture in figure 1.4 provides the schema that unlocks the meaning of the paragraph.

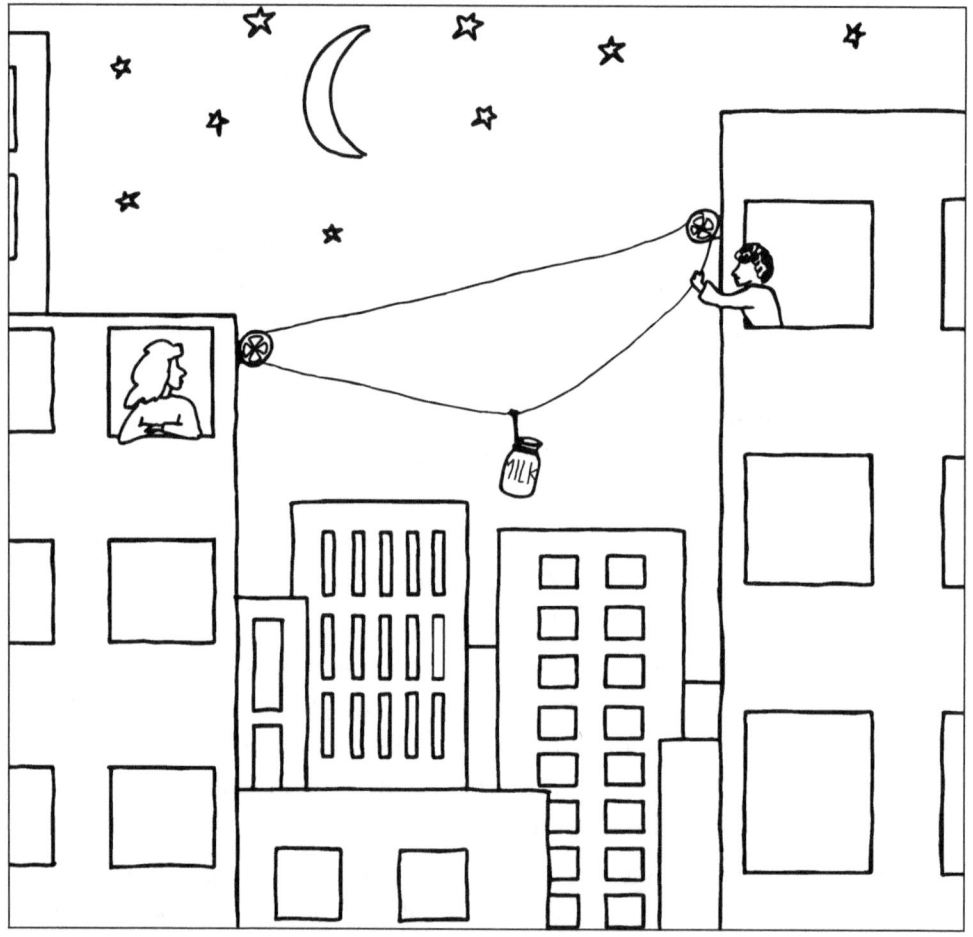

Source: Marzano, Dodson, et al., 2022, p. 170.
FIGURE 1.4: Schema picture.

Certainly, this passage is contrived, as its schema-generating picture illustrates. But together, they make an important point: If you don't have a schema for what you are reading, hearing, or seeing, you cannot make sense of it. Similarly, if students don't have schemas for the types of items they encounter in tests, they will likely answer those items incorrectly, even though they know the content that is the focus of those items. The rather glaring conclusion of these facts is that schools should make efforts to ensure that students are familiar with the schemas—which we more simply call *item frames* for the remainder of the book—of the items that will be used to assess their competence. Ultimately, that is the goal of this book.

SUMMARY

This chapter introduced and demonstrated the nature of test-specific thinking using an elementary language arts reading item and an elementary mathematics item. Even relatively simple items at lower grade levels like these commonly require thinking that is not related to the content being tested. The structure of the item itself often adds considerable difficulty to the task. The multiple-choice format is one important example particularly because it is used in so many types of tests for so many different content areas. This chapter also made the case that test-specific thinking is related to many of the thinking skills recommended in standards documents for various subject areas. Finally, this chapter connected the concept of test-specific thinking to the concept of schema. In effect, the unique thinking required of students on tests is a type of schema they must understand to demonstrate their mastery of the academic content on such tests. In the next few chapters, we explore schemas for ELA and mathematics and their use in classrooms.

CHAPTER 2

CONNECTING ELA ITEM FRAMES TO ACADEMIC CONTENT

This chapter begins our investigation of how schools can integrate test-specific thinking into their instructional programs by discussing the types of schemas that are prevalent in ELA test items. To effectively teach students about the test-specific thinking required to answer ELA items, educators must first be aware of the types of items found on external assessments and how they relate to the content they teach. To this end, we draw on *Ethical Test Preparation in the Classroom* (Marzano, Dodson, et al., 2022), which summarized the findings from an analysis of 8,800 items in ELA, mathematics, and science from state, national, and international tests. (These are collectively known as *large-scale assessments*, a term we will continue to use for the remainder of this book in lieu of terms like *external assessments*, *state assessments*, *end-of-year assessments*, and the like.) In that study, the authors analyzed 1,684 ELA items and organized those items into three broad categories: reading, language, and writing. Table 2.1 (page 18) depicts the frequency at which these three types of items appear across the grade levels.

One of the more salient findings reported in table 2.1 (page 18) is that 83 percent of the ELA items analyzed dealt with reading. Thus, a school leader or teacher might infer that instruction on reading items should be a major focus across all grade levels. Table 2.2 (page 18) depicts some other important general findings about item types.

Table 2.2 (page 18) is organized into two main categories of item types: selected-response items and constructed-response items. It is also organized by the three ELA domains: reading, language, and writing. These findings, combined with those in table 2.1 (page 18), can help sharpen the focus of ELA educators. Table 2.1 indicates that 83 percent of all items deal with reading, and table 2.2 indicates that 80 percent

TABLE 2.1: General Findings From ELA Study

	READING	LANGUAGE	WRITING	TOTAL	PERCENTAGE OF ITEMS
Grade 3	94	5	10	109	6
Grade 4	156	6	19	181	11
Grade 5	119	5	13	137	8
Grade 6	166	6	14	186	11
Grade 7	121	5	11	137	8
Grade 8	145	5	15	165	10
Grade 9	148	0	13	161	10
Grade 10	129	0	9	138	8
Grade 11	204	4	18	226	13
Grade 12 (NAEP)	25	0	6	31	2
SAT	52	44	1	97	6
ACT	40	75	1	116	7
Total	1,399	155	130	1,684	100
Percentage of Items	83	9	8	100	

Source: Marzano, Dodson, et al., 2022, p. 24.

TABLE 2.2: General Findings by Item Types

ITEM TYPE	DOMAIN	NUMBER OF ITEMS	PERCENTAGE OF ITEMS
Selected response	Reading	1,344	80
	Language	155	9
Short constructed response	Reading	55	3
Extended constructed response	Writing	130	8
Total		1,684	

Source: Marzano, Dodson, et al., 2022, p. 24.

of reading items are selected response. This is particularly interesting in light of the fact that there are actually twenty-five content topics addressed in ELA items, as follows (Marzano, Dodson, et al., 2022). One might not expect that a test involving so many different topics and types of item formats would be dominated by a small number of topics and one particular item format in terms of frequency of occurrence.

Selected Response: Reading
1. Big idea
2. Meaning
3. Detail
4. Evidence
5. Function
6. Purpose

Selected Response: Language—Content
7. Addition
8. Appropriate placement
9. Deletion

Selected Response: Language—Expressions
10. Relationships
11. Vocabulary
12. Word choice

Selected Response: Language—Grammar
13. Agreement
14. Sentence structure
15. Modifier placement and formation
16. Pronoun usage
17. Verb tense

Selected Response: Language—Mechanics
18. Capitalization
19. Punctuation
20. Spelling

Extended Constructed Response
21. Analytic
22. Argumentative
23. Comparative
24. Informational
25. Narrative

For each of these twenty-five types of items, *Ethical Test Preparation in the Classroom* (Marzano, Dodson, et al., 2022) articulated the basic format of the item along with the specific content that is the focus of the item. This book refers to these constructs as *item frames*. Schools and districts can use these item frames to make students aware of the schemas for all the ELA items on large-scale assessments rather than having them identify schemas on their own. In effect, the item frames described in *Ethical Test Preparation in the Classroom* are the tools educators can use to teach and reinforce various item schemas. Stated differently, item frames are vehicles for teaching and reinforcing test-specific thinking.

In the remainder of this chapter, we consider different ways that educators might connect item frames to daily learning in ELA.

MATCHING ITEM FRAMES TO STANDARDS

One way that a school can embed item frames into day-to-day activities is to match the frames to their standards. To illustrate, consider the following ELA standards from the state of Colorado for reading, writing, and communicating (Colorado Academic Standards, 2019b):

> Apply strategies to comprehend and interpret literary texts.
>   a. Use Key Ideas and Details to:
>   i. Refer to details and examples in a text when explaining what the text says explicitly and when drawing inferences from the text. (CCSS: RL.4.1)
>   ii. Determine a theme of a story, drama, or poem from details in the text; summarize the text. (CCSS: RL.4.2)
>   iii. Describe in depth a character, setting, or event in a story or drama, drawing on specific details in the text (for example: a character's thoughts, words, or actions). (CCSS: RL.4.3)
>   iv. Describe the development of plot (such as the origin of the central conflict, the action of the plot, and how the conflict is resolved).

Apply strategies to comprehend and interpret informational texts.
  a. Use Key Ideas and Details to:
      i. Refer to details and examples in a text when explaining what the text says explicitly and when drawing inferences from the text. (CCSS: RI.4.1)
      ii. Determine the main idea of a text and explain how it is supported by key details; summarize the text. (CCSS: RI.4.2)
      iii. Explain events, procedures, ideas, or concepts in a historical, scientific, or technical text, including what happened and why, based on specific information in the text. (CCSS: RI.4.3)

These standards refer to the skills of using key ideas and details with two types of texts: literary and informational. For both types of texts, element *i* of the standard requires students to use details and examples from the text when talking about the inferences they have made. When examining the various item frames listed on pages 19–20, one finds that detail frames are one of the six types found in the category of selected-response reading items. Consequently, this item frame can be used to directly teach and reinforce one of the skills in the Colorado state standards.

To illustrate, consider the sample detail item in figure 2.1. Assume that students have read passages from the book *Phillis's Big Test* by Catherine Clinton (2008). It is a story about Phillis Wheatley, who published a book of poetry in 1773. It was a great accomplishment that made her very famous. Only a year before, however, Phillis was required to take a test to prove that she was the actual author of these poems because she was enslaved, and many people did not believe an enslaved person could have written them.

Part A
What is the difference between Phillis's audience at the Wheatley home and the men at the exam?
  a. The Wheatley audience reads her poetry before she recites it.
  b. The men at the exam require her to prove herself.
  c. The Wheatley audience includes highly educated people.
  d. The men at the exam are greater in number.

Part B
Which paragraph from *Phillis's Big Test* provides evidence to support the answer to part A?
  a. Paragraph 11
  b. Paragraph 13
  c. Paragraph 15
  d. Paragraph 16

FIGURE 2.1: Sample detail item at the fifth-grade level.

This item frame has the following characteristics (Marzano, Dodson, et al., 2022): There are two questions to the item—part A and part B. Part A requires the test taker to answer a question involving details from a passage by selecting the correct answer from a list of alternatives. Part B requires the test taker to find evidence from the text that supports the answer that they selected in part A.

Ethical Test Preparation in the Classroom (Marzano, Dodson, et al., 2022) also provided directions for how classroom teachers can create items using the item frames. This is depicted in figure 2.2, continuing the example of detail frames.

---

1. Select a text that includes a great deal of detail, including examples and illustrations.
2. Write part A using one of the following stems.
    a. According to the text, who, what, when, where, why, or how?
    b. Based on the text, who, what, when, where, why, or how?
3. Create a correct choice.
4. Create alternative choices that are incorrect.
5. Write part B using one of the following stems.
    a. What evidence best supports the answer to part A?
    b. What information best supports the answer to part A?
6. Create a correct choice.
7. Create alternative choices that are incorrect.

Source: Marzano, Dodson, et al., 2022, p. 33.
FIGURE 2.2: Directions for creating detail items.

Using these directions provides teachers with an experiential understanding of the basic schema for a selected-response detail item. In effect, as teachers create items using directions like those in figure 2.2, they develop an understanding of the schemas for those items, which they can then pass on to students.

MATCHING ITEM FRAMES TO THE CURRICULUM

Another way to use item frames in the classroom is to match them to specific parts of the curriculum. This can be accomplished by examining the contents of textbooks or programs used in the school. For example, an elementary school using a specific ELA program might examine the various modules into which the program is organized. Educators find that one of the modules at the fifth-grade level highlights the topic of subject-verb agreement. Scanning the list of item types on pages 19–20, teachers see that there are specific item frames for this aspect of ELA. A sample item for this topic is depicted in figure 2.3.

> Read the following sentence and select the word that is most appropriate for the sentence.
>
> > The major leagues in European soccer, which represents much of soccer's worldwide leadership, _____ unilaterally defended the coach's move to bench the veteran center-back player.
>
> Which word completes the sentence correctly?
>   a. are
>   b. has
>   c. have
>   d. will

FIGURE 2.3: Sample item for subject-verb agreement.

The teachers then use the directions for creating items for this topic from *Ethical Test Preparation in the Classroom* (Marzano, Dodson, et al., 2022), which are depicted in figure 2.4. These directions highlight the fact that items of this type require students to think more in terms of *editing* a sentence for subject-verb agreement than *creating* a sentence that has correct subject-verb agreement.

> 1. Pick a passage or a sentence in a text that contains a clear subject and a predicate.
> 2. Leave a blank in the space where the predicate is.
> 3. Write a correct option.
> 4. Write two or three incorrect options.

Source: Adapted from Marzano, Dodson, et al., 2022.
FIGURE 2.4: Directions for creating items for subject-verb agreement.

MATCHING ITEM FRAMES TO COMMON ASSESSMENTS

Common assessments have been a staple in many classrooms since the early 2000s. In their book, *Common Formative Assessments: How to Connect Standards-Based Instruction and Assessment*, Larry Ainsworth and Donald Viegut (2006) chronicled the development of common assessments and attested to their importance in the ongoing monitoring of student learning. In brief, *common assessments* are assessments that groups of teachers who are teaching the same content at the same time jointly develop, administer, and score. Such groups are referred to as *collaborative teams*. Richard DuFour, Rebecca DuFour, Robert Eaker, and Thomas Many (2010) made common assessment an integral part of the PLC process:

> Instead of individual teachers developing and administering a summative test at the end of a unit, a collaborative team of teachers responsible for the same course or grade level creates a common *formative* assessment before teaching a unit. Members of the team agree on the standard students must achieve to be deemed proficient and establish when they will give the assessment. (p. 208)

DuFour and his colleagues (2010) went on to explain that immediately after a common assessment is administered, members of the collaborative team analyze the results to determine appropriate actions they can take in class. Thus, the common assessment provides focused data used by team members to optimize their instructional effectiveness.

Item frames fit rather nicely into this process. Specifically, when a team decides on a topic of focus for a common assessment, they look for the frame or frames that best fit that topic and embed the items in the test. For example, assume a team of ELA teachers is developing a common assessment regarding the use of expressions. Consulting *Ethical Test Preparation in the Classroom* (Marzano, Dodson, et al., 2022), the team notes that there are specific item frames on this topic. One such item is depicted in figure 2.5.

A student is writing a report about her experience learning to ride a horse. Read the draft of the report and complete the task that follows.

> When I met Chestnut, she was very timid. My instructor helped me climb into the saddle, and Chestnut whinnied and tossed her head. I was worried Chestnut didn't like me very much. Eventually, she calmed down, and we started to walk slowly around the corral. After I got used to riding slowly, my instructor tried to get Chestnut to trot faster, but Chestnut just kept walking. My instructor said Chestnut would have to learn to trust me. It was disappointing that I did not get to ride Chestnut very fast. _____, learning to ride a horse has been very interesting so far.

Choose the **best two** phrases to connect "It was disappointing that I did not get to ride Chestnut very fast" and "learning to ride a horse has been very interesting so far."

☐ Even so
☐ Later on
☐ Let alone
☐ Despite this
☐ For example
☐ In other words

Source: Marzano, Dodson, et al., 2022, p. 55.

FIGURE 2.5: Expressions item.

This example not only provides a format for the collaborative team to use when designing the items on its common assessment, but it also lets the team members know that they should make students aware of the fact that they must navigate items that present more than one correct answer when they are taking large-scale assessments.

MATCHING ITEM FRAMES TO PROFICIENCY SCALES

Proficiency scales have been used in K–12 education since the 1990s (Marzano & Kendall, 1996). They are statements of knowledge and skill for specific topics organized into a learning progression. Proficiency scales make a school's curriculum transparent to teachers, students, parents, and guardians. They make explicit what students must do to demonstrate proficiency as well as the continuum of knowledge and skill leading up to and exceeding proficiency. For example, figure 2.6 displays a proficiency scale for the topic of "analyzing the development of an idea or theme over the course of a text." This is a topic that might be taught in a ninth-grade ELA class.

4.0	In addition to score 3.0 performance, the student demonstrates in-depth inferences and applications that go beyond what was taught.
3.5	In addition to score 3.0 performance, partial success at score 4.0 content
3.0	The student can analyze the development of an idea or theme over the course of a text through details (for example, explain which details are the most important in developing the idea of reputation throughout Arthur Miller's *The Crucible*).
2.5	No major errors or omissions regarding score 2.0 content, and partial success at score 3.0 content

2.0	The student understands basic information like the following.
	• Details might be small, but they are often integral to the text. *Who, what, where, when, why,* and *how* questions are common detail types, but questions that focus on detail also focus on the specific structure of the test. For example, the following structures are often accompanied by the kinds of detail questions listed.
	  • Important aspects of textual arguments (for example, *who* questions about people important to the argument; *what* questions about the content of the argument; *where* questions about places relevant to the argument; *when* questions about the time frame relevant to the argument; *why* questions about the necessity of the argument)
	  • Important aspects of complex cause and effect (for example, questions about who was involved in the cause-and-effect structure; what occurred as a result of the cause-and-effect relationship; where

FIGURE 2.6: Grade 9 ELA proficiency scale.   continued →

		the cause-and-effect relationship occurred; when the cause-and-effect relationship occurred; why the cause-and-effect relationship occurred; how the cause-and-effect relationship occurred) • Important aspects of plots with complex problems that do not have satisfactory solutions (for example, questions about who was involved in the problem or solution; what occurred to create the problem or solution; where the problem or solution occurred; when the problem or solution occurred; why the problem or solution occurred; how things occurred during the problem or solution) • Important aspects of plots with multiple storylines (for example, questions about who was involved in various phases of the plot; what occurred during various phases of the plot; where various phases of the plot occurred; when various phases of the plot occurred; why various phases of the plot occurred; how various phases of the plot occurred)
	1.5	Partial success at score 2.0 content, and major errors or omissions regarding score 3.0 content
	1.0	With help, partial success at score 2.0 content and score 3.0 content
	0.5	With help, partial success at score 2.0 content but not at score 3.0 content
	0.0	Even with help, no success

Source: © 2016 by Marzano Resources. Adapted with permission.

The content at score 3.0 of a proficiency scale represents expectations for student performance. In this case, the expectation is that students can analyze the development of an idea or theme over the course of a text through details. The score 2.0 content represents information students should know to accomplish the 3.0 expectations. Notice that the score 2.0 content presents students with very granular information about the nature of details in different types of texts. Score 4.0 of a proficiency scale includes a general expectation that students can make inferences and applications that go beyond score 3.0 expectations. Scale values 1.0 and 0.0 address what students can and cannot do with help. Between the whole-point values on the scale are half-point values signifying partial acquisition of the content at the next level up on the scale. For detailed descriptions of how such scales are developed and used, see *Making Classroom Assessments Reliable and Valid* (Marzano, 2018) or *The New Art and Science of Classroom Assessment* (Marzano, Norford, & Ruyle, 2019).

Item frames can easily be used as complements to proficiency scales. Specifically, item frames can be used to structure tasks at score 3.0 of a scale. Again, the first step is to identify the item frame or frames that most closely fit the content in the proficiency scale. The proficiency scale in figure 2.6 clearly focuses on details in a text. Consequently, the detail item frame in reading is a good complement to this proficiency. A sample detail item is provided in figure 2.7.

Part A

Which statement **best** describes the main difference between Gwen and Miss Roscoe in the passage from *The Youngest Girl in the Fifth*?

    a. Gwen takes time to think, while Miss Roscoe acts quickly.
    b. Gwen seems to be timid, while Miss Roscoe appears to be daring.
    c. Gwen likes to dream, while Miss Roscoe prefers facts.
    d. Gwen wants things to remain the same, while Miss Roscoe seeks change.

Part B

Which **two** details from the passage support the answer to part A?

    a. "quailed alike under the glance of her keen dark eyes" (paragraph 1)
    b. "stood hesitating near the door" (paragraph 2)
    c. "you ought to be able to manage the work" (paragraph 2)
    d. "With that help you shouldn't be so far behind" (paragraph 4)
    e. "wished she could have had a little time to get accustomed" (paragraph 7)
    f. "she never had a moment to waste" (paragraph 7)

FIGURE 2.7: Sample detail item to be used with *The Youngest Girl in the Fifth* by Angela Brazil.

Given that students were reading *The Youngest Girl in the Fifth*, a teacher could use this item frame to determine students' competence at score 3.0 of the proficiency scale. Additionally, the teacher would present students with some strategies for addressing the test-specific thinking necessary to navigate such items.

INTEGRATING ITEM FRAMES INTO PROFICIENCY SCALES

Going a step further in the integration of proficiency scales and item frames, if districts or schools wish to standardize the use of item frames within their curriculum, they can create proficiency scales that explicitly include item frames with which students might demonstrate proficiency at score 3.0. To illustrate, consider figure 2.8.

4.0	The student can create their own version of the item-frame task and then: • Modify their version to make it easier, and explain why the modification works • Modify their version to make it more difficult, and explain why the modification works
3.5	In addition to score 3.0 performance, partial success at score 4.0 content
3.0	The student can analyze the development of an idea or theme over the course of a text through details, especially in the context of items like the following.

FIGURE 2.8: Proficiency scale with embedded item frame.   continued →

Part A

Which statement **best** describes the main difference between Gwen and Miss Roscoe in the passage from *The Youngest Girl in the Fifth*?

   a. Gwen takes time to think, while Miss Roscoe acts quickly.
   b. Gwen seems to be timid, while Miss Roscoe appears to be daring.
   c. Gwen likes to dream, while Miss Roscoe prefers facts.
   d. Gwen wants things to remain the same, while Miss Roscoe seeks change.

Part B

Which **two** details from the passage support the answer to part A?

   a. "quailed alike under the glance of her keen dark eyes" (paragraph 1)
   b. "stood hesitating near the door" (paragraph 2)
   c. "you ought to be able to manage the work" (paragraph 2)
   d. "you shouldn't be so far behind" (paragraph 4)
   e. "wished she could have had a little time to get accustomed" (paragraph 7)
   f. "she never had a moment to waste" (paragraph 7)

The student directly answers such items independently.

Additionally, the student can describe a reasonable strategy for addressing items of this type. Such a strategy might be a unique creation of the student's, or it might contain information presented to the student about:

- The content important for item success
- The item type

2.5	No major errors or omissions regarding score 2.0 content, and partial success at score 3.0 content

2.0	The student understands the content elements necessary for item success. Specifically, the student knows:
	
	• Details might be small, but they are often integral to the text. *Who, what, where, when, why,* and *how* questions are common detail types, but questions that focus on detail also focus on the specific structure of the test. For example, the following structures are often accompanied by the kinds of detail questions listed.
	   • Important aspects of textual arguments (for example, *who* questions about people important to the argument; *what* questions about the content of the argument; *where* questions about places relevant to the argument; *when* questions about the time frame relevant to the argument; *why* questions about the necessity of the argument)
	   • Important aspects of complex cause and effect (for example, questions about who was involved in the cause-and-effect structure; what occurred as a result of the cause-and-effect relationship; where the cause-and-effect relationship occurred; when the cause-and-effect relationship occurred; why the cause-and-effect relationship occurred; how the cause-and-effect relationship occurred)
	   • Important aspects of plots with complex problems that do not have satisfactory solutions (for example, questions about who was involved in the problem or solution; what occurred to create the

		problem or solution; where the problem or solution occurred; when the problem or solution occurred; why the problem or solution occurred; how things occurred during the problem or solution)
• Important aspects of plots with multiple storylines (for example, questions about who was involved in various phases of the plot; what occurred during various phases of the plot; where various phases of the plot occurred; when various phases of the plot occurred; why various phases of the plot occurred; how various phases of the plot occurred)
	1.5	Partial success at score 2.0 content, and major errors or omissions regarding score 3.0 content
	1.0	With help, partial success at score 2.0 content and score 3.0 content
	0.5	With help, partial success at score 2.0 content but not at score 3.0 content
	0.0	Even with help, no success

Notice that score 3.0 of this proficiency scale provides a sample item that would demonstrate proficiency if students could correctly navigate it. This represents a shift from the traditional form of a proficiency scale depicted in figure 2.6 (page 25), where score 3.0 contains a general description of expected student performance ("Analyze the development of an idea or theme over the course of a text through details").

This shift moves proficiency scales into the realm of instructional objectives, which were introduced to educators in the early 1960s. In the book *Preparing Instructional Objectives*, Robert F. Mager (1962), an influential psychologist, defined *instructional objectives* in a very specific manner. According to Mager, a well-written objective includes three main components.

1. **Performance:** This specifies what the learner is expected to do to demonstrate that they have achieved the objective. It should be an observable and measurable action or behavior.

    - *Example*—"The student will be able to identify errors of subject-verb agreement."

2. **Conditions:** These describe the conditions under which the performance is to occur. These include the tools, materials, or circumstances that will be provided to the learner.

    - *Example*—"Given a set of twenty sentences, ten of which have errors of subject-verb agreement, . . ."

3. **Criterion:** This specifies the level of performance that will be considered acceptable. It sets the standard for how well the learner must perform the task.

    - *Example*—". . . with 90 percent accuracy."

Mager asserted that together, these components ensure that objectives are clear, specific, and measurable, which helps both teachers and learners understand what is expected and how success will be assessed. Since their inception, instructional objectives have been used in a wide variety of fields, such as medicine (Chatterjee & Corral, 2017).

It's important to note that in the proficiency scale that includes an explicit item frame (figure 2.8, page 27), the 3.0 expectation is that students can describe a reasonable strategy for addressing items of this type. Such a strategy might be a student's unique creation, or it might contain information presented to the student about the content important for success and the item type. At score 4.0, the expectation is that students can create their own version of the item-frame task and then: (1) modify their version to make it easier, and explain why the modification works, and (2) modify their version to make it more difficult, and explain why the modification works. In effect, the type of proficiency scale depicted in figure 2.8 integrates the teaching of item frames and test-specific thinking into instruction in academic content.

FOCUSING ON HIGH-FREQUENCY ITEM FRAMES

One approach to teaching ELA item frames is to employ frames for all twenty-five types of items listed on pages 19–20. Another approach is to focus on the frames that appear with the highest frequency in large-scale assessments, at least at the beginning of an item-frame initiative. An examination of the study reported in *Ethical Test Preparation in the Classroom* (Marzano, Dodson, et al., 2022) disclosed some clear patterns. For one, the vast majority of ELA items on large-scale assessments are selected-response reading items. Another pattern is that most selected-response reading items have two parts. In these situations, students first respond to an item regarding the passage they have just read. They then respond to a second item based on their response to the first item. The distribution of selected-response reading items with one or more parts is depicted in table 2.3.

TABLE 2.3: Distribution of Selected-Response Reading Items With One, Two, or Three Parts

NUMBER OF PARTS	NUMBER OF ITEMS	PERCENTAGE OF TOTAL ITEMS
One-Part Items (part A only)	333	24.78
Two-Part Items (parts A and B only)	1,005	74.78
Three-Part Items (parts A, B, and C)	6	0.45
Total	1,344	

Note: Percentages do not sum to 100 due to rounding.

Source: Marzano, Dodson, et al., 2022, p. 27.

According to table 2.3, almost 75 percent of selected-response reading items have two parts, with only about 25 percent involving one part and less than 1 percent involving three parts. Clearly, two-part selected-response reading items represent the vast majority of selected-response reading item types.

A final pattern to consider from the study involves the nature of the part B items. As depicted in table 2.4, 70.25 percent of the items in the part B section of selected-response reading items involve students providing evidence from the text for their answers in the part A section.

TABLE 2.4: Reading Frames in Selected-Response Items (Part B)

FRAME	NUMBER OF ITEMS	PERCENTAGE OF ITEMS	MOST COMMON STEMS
Evidence	706	70.25	What evidence or information (best) supports the answer to part A (the previous question)?
Function	145	14.43	Which [Textual Element] does [Literary Element]?
Meaning	115	11.44	Which information helps the reader understand the meaning of a word or phrase?
Detail	19	1.89	According to or based on the text, [Who, What, When, Where, Why, or How]?
Big Idea	18	1.79	Which sentences, details, or paragraphs belong in, relate to, or provide a summary of the text?
Purpose	2	0.20	What is the purpose of [Textual Element]?
Total	1,005	100	

Source: Marzano, Dodson, et al., 2022, p. 28.

Combining all results regarding ELA items, one can draw the conclusion that the most common skills addressed in large-scale assessments are the following.

- Determining the main idea
- Determining the meaning of specific words and phrases
- Determining how the details in a text contribute to its messages
- Determining how specific rhetorical devices influence the meaning of the text
- Determining the purpose for which the text was written
- Determining evidence for specific conclusions

Additionally, the most common type of item found on ELA tests has the format depicted in figure 2.9. This general format is ubiquitous across the items dealing with reading comprehension.

SUMMARY

This chapter presented twenty-five categories of ELA item frames identified in the study of 1,684 ELA test items on state, national, and international tests reported in *Ethical Test Preparation in the Classroom* (Marzano, Dodson, et al., 2022). Educators can and should embed these item frames into the day-to-day activities of schooling. This chapter focused on four different ways these item frames can be integrated into regular classroom instruction: (1) matching item frames to standards, (2) matching item frames to the curriculum, (3) matching item frames to common assessments, and (4) matching item frames to proficiency scales. Additionally, in this chapter, we provided an example of how item frames can be directly embedded in proficiency scales. Finally, we discussed putting an emphasis on the types of items that students are likely to encounter most frequently. This chapter provided educators with the foundational knowledge for how they might use ELA item frames in their classrooms. The next chapter addresses specific ways to integrate ELA item frames into instruction.

In 1960, while campaigning to be elected president, Senator John F. Kennedy gave a speech at the University of Michigan in which he proposed the idea of an international service organization that would become the Peace Corps. Read the speech from Senator Kennedy below and answer the questions that follow.

Remarks of Senator John F. Kennedy

I want to express my thanks to you, as a graduate of the Michigan of the East, Harvard University.

I come here tonight delighted to have the opportunity to say one or two words about this campaign that is coming into the last three weeks.

I think in many ways it is the most important campaign since 1933, mostly because of the problems which press upon the United States, and the opportunities which will be presented to us in the 1960s. The opportunity must be seized, through the judgment of the President, and the vigor of the executive, and the cooperation of the Congress. Through these I think we can make the greatest possible difference.

How many of you who are going to be doctors, are willing to spend your days in Ghana? Technicians or engineers, how many of you are willing to work in the Foreign Service and spend your lives traveling around the world? On your willingness to do that, not merely to serve one year or two years in the service, but on your willingness to contribute part of your life to this country, I think will depend the answer whether a free society can compete. I think it can! And I think Americans are willing to contribute. But the effort must be far greater than we have ever made in the past.

Therefore, I am delighted to come to Michigan, to this university, because unless we have those resources in this school, unless you comprehend the nature of what is being asked of you, this country can't possibly move through the next 10 years in a period of relative strength.

So I come here tonight to go to bed! But I also come here tonight to ask you to join in the effort . . .

This university . . . this is the longest short speech I've ever made . . . therefore, I'll finish it! Let me say in conclusion, this University is not maintained by its alumni, or by the state, merely to help its graduates have an economic advantage in the life struggle. There is certainly a greater purpose, and I'm sure you recognize it. Therefore, I do not apologize for asking for your support in this campaign. I come here tonight asking your support for this country over the next decade.

Thank you.

Senator John F. Kennedy

October 14, 1960

Part A

What is a central idea of Senator Kennedy's speech?
  a. A college education can help people get better jobs and careers.
  b. The executive and legislative branches are the most important parts of the government.
  c. People should vote for Senator Kennedy for president.
  d. Americans should use their knowledge and skills to serve their country.

Part B

What evidence best supports the answer to part A?
  a. "On your willingness to do that, not merely to serve one year or two years in the service, but on your willingness to contribute part of your life to this country, I think will depend the answer whether a free society can compete."
  b. "Therefore, I do not apologize for asking for your support in this campaign."
  c. "The opportunity must be seized, through the judgment of the President, and the vigor of the executive, and the cooperation of the Congress. Through these I think we can make the greatest possible difference."
  d. "Let me say in conclusion, this University is not maintained by its alumni, or by the state, merely to help its graduates have an economic advantage in the life struggle."

Source for speech: Peace Corps, n.d.

FIGURE 2.9: Most common type of item found on ELA tests.

CHAPTER 3

USING ELA ITEM FRAMES IN CLASSROOM INSTRUCTION

With selected item frames matched to the standards, curriculum, common assessments, or proficiency scales, teachers should never be in doubt as to which item frames to use for a given set of lessons or unit of study. Additionally, teachers need clear guidance as to how to use the item frames. This chapter presents three steps involved in using item frames effectively.

1. Teach the content that is the focus of the item frame.
2. Present students with potential strategies for approaching the item.
3. Provide students with multiple opportunities to analyze items.

The following sections explain each step.

STEP 1: TEACH THE CONTENT THAT IS THE FOCUS OF THE ITEM FRAME

The first step when using item frames is to teach the content the item is designed to assess. Ideally, this content is explicated in a proficiency scale the school has created. As described in the previous chapter, we recommend that schools develop proficiency scales with embedded item frames. To illustrate, reconsider the proficiency scale for the topic of analyzing the development of an idea through the use of detail, introduced in the previous chapter and shown again in figure 3.1 (page 36).

The score 2.0 elements in the proficiency scale represent the foundational content that students should be taught directly. For this topic, that content includes information about the various types of details that might be important in a text. Such information includes the following.

- Details are small but important parts of texts.
- Details are the answers to *who, what, where, when, why,* and *how* questions.

4.0	The student can create their own version of the item-frame task and then: • Modify their version to make it easier, and explain why the modification works • Modify their version to make it more difficult, and explain why the modification works
3.5	In addition to score 3.0 performance, partial success at score 4.0 content

3.0	The student can analyze the development of an idea or theme over the course of a text through details, especially in the context of items like the following.
	
	Part A
	Which statement **best** describes the main difference between Gwen and Miss Roscoe in the passage from *The Youngest Girl in the Fifth*?
	   a. Gwen takes time to think, while Miss Roscoe acts quickly.
	   b. Gwen seems to be timid, while Miss Roscoe appears to be daring.
	   c. Gwen likes to dream, while Miss Roscoe prefers facts.
	   d. Gwen wants things to remain the same, while Miss Roscoe seeks change.
	
	Part B
	Which **two** details from the passage support the answer to part A?
	   a. "quailed alike under the glance of her keen dark eyes" (paragraph 1)
	   b. "stood hesitating near the door" (paragraph 2)
	   c. "you ought to be able to manage the work" (paragraph 2)
	   d. "you shouldn't be so far behind" (paragraph 4)
	   e. "wished she could have had a little time to get accustomed" (paragraph 7)
	   f. "she never had a moment to waste" (paragraph 7)
	
	Additionally, the student can describe a reasonable strategy for addressing items of this type. Such a strategy might be a unique creation of the student's, or it might contain information presented to the student about:
	• The content important for item success
	• The item type

2.5	No major errors or omissions regarding score 2.0 content, and partial success at score 3.0 content
2.0	The student understands the content elements necessary for item success. Specifically, the student knows: • Details might be small, but they are often integral to the text. *Who, what, where, when, why,* and *how* questions are common detail types, but questions that focus on detail also focus on the specific structure of the test. For example, the following structures are often accompanied by the kinds of detail questions listed. ◦ Important aspects of textual arguments (for example, *who* questions about people important to the argument; *what* questions about the content of the argument; *where* questions about places relevant to the argument; *when* questions about the time frame relevant to the argument; *why* questions about the necessity of the argument)

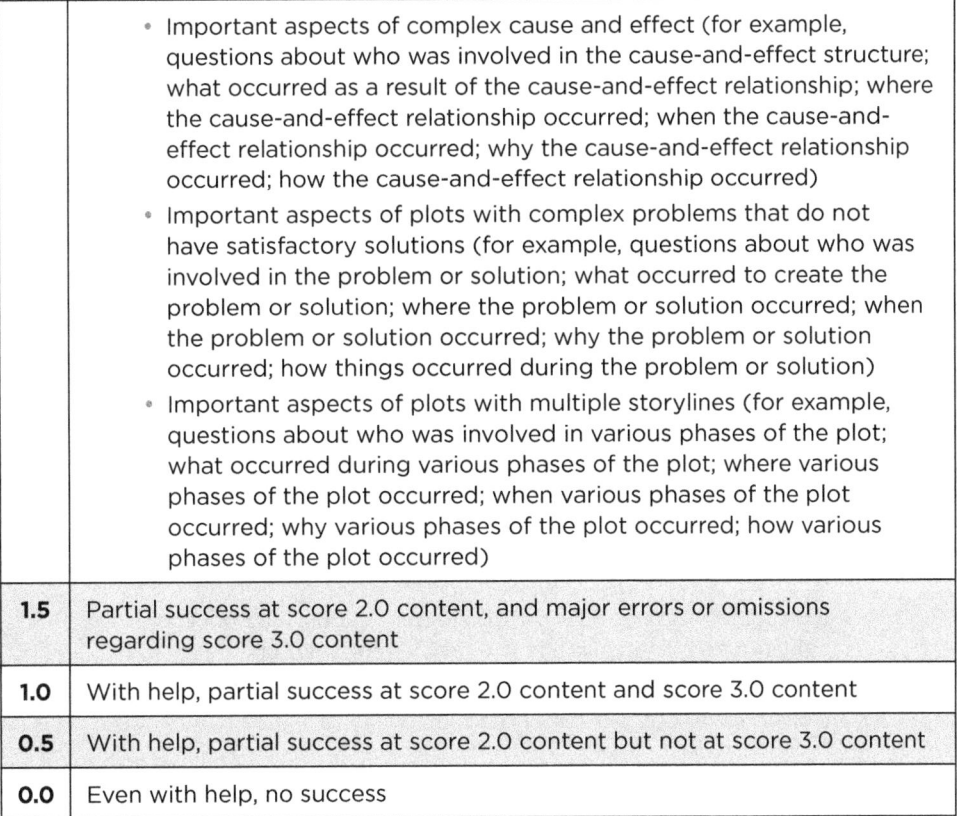

	• Important aspects of complex cause and effect (for example, questions about who was involved in the cause-and-effect structure; what occurred as a result of the cause-and-effect relationship; where the cause-and-effect relationship occurred; when the cause-and-effect relationship occurred; why the cause-and-effect relationship occurred; how the cause-and-effect relationship occurred) • Important aspects of plots with complex problems that do not have satisfactory solutions (for example, questions about who was involved in the problem or solution; what occurred to create the problem or solution; where the problem or solution occurred; when the problem or solution occurred; why the problem or solution occurred; how things occurred during the problem or solution) • Important aspects of plots with multiple storylines (for example, questions about who was involved in various phases of the plot; what occurred during various phases of the plot; where various phases of the plot occurred; when various phases of the plot occurred; why various phases of the plot occurred; how various phases of the plot occurred)
1.5	Partial success at score 2.0 content, and major errors or omissions regarding score 3.0 content
1.0	With help, partial success at score 2.0 content and score 3.0 content
0.5	With help, partial success at score 2.0 content but not at score 3.0 content
0.0	Even with help, no success

FIGURE 3.1: Proficiency scale with embedded item frame.

- *Who*, *what*, *where*, *when*, *why*, and *how* questions have different emphases in different types of texts, such as argument, complex cause and effect, plots with complex problems that do not have satisfactory solutions, or plots with multiple storylines.
- For argument texts, *who* questions are about the people who are important to the claim or support the claim.
- For complex cause and effect, *who* questions are about the people involved in the cause or consequence of an event.
- For plots that do not have satisfactory solutions, *who* questions are about the people involved in the problem or solution.
- For plots with multiple storylines, *who* questions are about the people involved in various phases of the plot.

To directly teach and exemplify this content to students, a teacher might first determine which content students already know, perhaps by administering a pretest regarding this content. Another option is to administer a brief survey regarding the 2.0 elements, like the one in figure 3.2 (page 38).

> Directions: Indicate how well you think you know each of the following pieces of information using the following scales.
>
>   1: I don't know this at all.
>   2: I know a little bit about this.
>   3: I understand this.
>
> ____ Details are small but important parts of texts.
>
> ____ Details are the answers to *who, what, where, when, why,* and *how* questions.
>
> ____ *Who, what, where, when, why,* and *how* questions have different emphases in different types of text, such as argument, complex cause and effect, plots with complex problems that do not have satisfactory solutions, or plots with multiple storylines.
>
> ____ For argument texts, *who* questions are about the people who are important to the claim or support the claim.
>
> ____ For complex cause and effect, *who* questions are about the people involved in the cause or consequence of an event.
>
> ____ For plots that do not have satisfactory solutions, *who* questions are about the people involved in the problem or solution.
>
> ____ For plots with multiple storylines, *who* questions are about the people involved in various phases of the plot.

FIGURE 3.2: Student survey of score 2.0 content.

For topics students do not know, the teacher provides appropriate direct instruction. For example, assume the teacher finds that a majority of students in class are not familiar with the types of details found in texts about complex causal relationships. The teacher thus provides a direct-instruction lesson where they present students with a passage in which specific causes and consequences are important aspects of the main idea. The teacher points out these details and engages students in a discussion of the evidence for the specific event in question. The teacher might also have students find examples of this type of detail in other texts and then create short texts of their own that have this type of detail.

STEP 2: PRESENT STUDENTS WITH POTENTIAL STRATEGIES FOR APPROACHING THE ITEM

Along with the content that pertains directly to an item, teachers should present students with information about the unique characteristics of the item type and various ways to potentially approach the item. For example, relative to the sample detail test item at score 3.0 of figure 3.1 (page 36), the teacher might present students with information like the following.

- As you read a text, try to notice the important things that are happening.
- It can be helpful to review the important things that happened when you are done reading.
- Read each item on the test and try to determine if it is asking a *who, what, where, when, why,* or *how* question about the story. Keep in mind that these detail questions might be about a cause-and-effect relationship, a chronology of events, a problem-solution situation, or a storyline.
- As you read the text, make annotations about the important details.

Notice that the proficiency scale in figure 3.1 (page 36) includes a specific item frame at score 3.0 but does not describe a specific strategy or set of strategies that should be taught to students. However, the proficiency scale does include the following language.

- Additionally, the student can describe a reasonable strategy for addressing items of this type. Such a strategy might be a unique creation of the student's, or it might contain information presented to the student about:
  - The content important for item success
  - The item type

In effect, at score 3.0 in the scale, students must not only be able to solve problems of a specific type but also have some awareness of the item type and what it requires of the test taker. The strategies and information the teacher shares with students for approaching this type of item and the pertinent content are the building blocks students use to craft their personal approach to addressing the item.

STEP 3: PROVIDE STUDENTS WITH MULTIPLE OPPORTUNITIES TO ANALYZE ITEMS

On a regular basis, students should be provided with multiple opportunities to interact with item frames that have been selected as the focus of instruction. But such interaction should go well beyond simply asking students to answer items as a form of practice. Rather, each encounter with an item should ask students to analyze the item type and their thinking regarding the item type. There are a number of ways to do this, which the following sections describe.

Teacher Alterations

One option to provide students with opportunities to analyze items and their own thinking about those items is for the teacher to present an item and then make alterations in the item. To illustrate, reconsider the item presented in chapter 1 (page 3) about cicadas. Recall that students first read a passage about cicadas and then answered the two-part question shown in figure 3.3.

Part A
What is the main idea of the text?
  a. Cicadas are very useful animals.
  b. Scientists know very little about cicadas.
  c. People in the past were not as smart as people are today.
  d. Cicadas are interesting, not frightening.

Part B
What evidence best supports the answer to part A?
  a. Then they mate and lay eggs.
  b. They had never seen cicadas before.
  c. In fact, scientists have found that cicadas do not hurt crops or plants.
  d. Some cicadas have come out ahead of schedule.

FIGURE 3.3: Two-part question for the passage about cicadas (figure 1.1, page 4).

The teacher would first provide students with time to answer this two-part question and then have them discuss their answers in small groups. The teacher might also lead a whole-class discussion of the item. After the discussion, the teacher would provide students with an altered version of the item, like the one in figure 3.4.

Part A
What is the main idea of the text?
  a. Cicadas are very useful animals.
  b. Scientists know very little about cicadas.
  c. People in the past were not as smart as people are today.
  d. Cicadas are interesting, not frightening.
  e. We still have a lot to learn about cicadas.

Part B
What evidence best supports the answer to part A?
  a. Then they mate and lay eggs.
  b. They had never seen cicadas before.
  c. In fact, scientists have found that cicadas do not hurt crops or plants.
  d. Some cicadas have come out ahead of schedule.
  e. Scientists are still trying to find out more about cicadas.

FIGURE 3.4: Altered item for the passage about cicadas.

Note that in figure 3.4, the teacher added a response option *e* for both part A and part B of the item. The teacher would ask students to analyze this new version of the item and determine whether it is easier or harder than the original version. Some students might say that because there are more options in the new version, there is more to consider in the item—therefore, it is more difficult. On further analysis, some of the students might notice that option *e* ("We still have a lot to learn about cicadas") in part A represents a viable answer to the main idea of the passage. Option *a* ("Cicadas are very useful animals") is still a major theme of the passage, but another emphasis in the passage is that "cicadas are interesting, not frightening" (option *d*). The students might note that this makes the item much more difficult because it is hard to determine whether option *a* is better than option *e* as the main idea of the passage. The item is more difficult, but not simply because there are more possible answers to consider. The teacher then would ask each student to summarize what they have learned about the content the item was designed to assess or the type of item itself. Some students might conclude that, if possible correct answers are very similar, it makes it much harder to determine the right answer.

Student Alterations

Another approach is for the teacher to present students with an item, have them answer the item, and then have them make their own alterations—as opposed to the teacher making the alteration in the item. More specifically, after students have answered an item, the teacher would ask them to make changes to the item and explain why their changes make the item harder or easier. Of course, this approach is most effective if students have had some experience with teacher-altered items. To illustrate student-altered items, first consider figure 3.5.

Kate shifted apprehensively as she waited to begin, but as she sprinted toward the platform and launched herself into the air, her worries fell away, and, flipping and twisting and soaring, she remembered the pure, unbridled joy that had made her fall in love with gymnastics in the first place.

How does the author's use of the phrase "worries fell away" help the reader understand Kate's experience as a gymnast?
   a. The phrase tells the reader that Kate has been doing gymnastics for a long time.
   b. The phrase shows the reader that Kate feels a lot of pressure to perform.
   c. The phrase emphasizes that Kate is a very skilled gymnast.
   d. The phrase indicates that Kate no longer enjoys gymnastics.

FIGURE 3.5: Seventh-grade function item.

Figure 3.5 (page 41) is a fairly straightforward function item in that it requires test takers to determine the function of a specific phrase in the passage. Students would first answer the item themselves and discuss which option is the best answer. In this case, the best answer is option *b*: "The phrase shows the reader that Kate feels a lot of pressure to perform." In their discussion, students might note that the mention of "pressure to perform" creates a link with the concept of worry explicit in the text and the item stem.

After students discuss the answer as provided in the item, they would then focus on making their own alterations to the item. For example, some students might focus on changing the provided multiple-choice options. One student might suggest that both the question and the alternatives can be changed to the following.

What does the author's use of apprehensively *in the first sentence tell the reader about Kate?*

  a. *The word tells the reader that Kate has been doing gymnastics for a long time.*
  b. *The word shows the reader that Kate is sometimes worried about her routine.*
  c. *The word emphasizes that Kate is a very skilled gymnast.*
  d. *The word indicates that Kate no longer enjoys gymnastics.*

After such alterations, the teacher would ask students to explain whether their changes make the item easier or harder. The student who made the preceding changes might explain that these changes make the item a little easier because *apprehensively* in the text and *worried* in the answer are very close to being synonyms.

Student-Generated Items

Still another option to help students analyze items is to have them create their own items for a particular frame, then alter their own items and describe why their alterations made their item easier or harder. Again, assume we are still dealing with the item about Kate and gymnastics. After students answer this item, the teacher would direct them to write their own item similar to the one about Kate.

Students would first have to identify the text that will be the focus of their item. The teacher might provide the text for students or allow them to select a text on their own. Next, the teacher would review the defining characteristics of the type of item on which students are focusing. Staying with the preceding examples, the teacher would remind students that a function item focuses on some rhetorical aspect of the text that plays an important role (that is, serves a specific function) in the text. The teacher might remind students that the element that performs this function can be a phrase or set of related terms (as evidenced in the text about Kate executing gymnastics moves). But it could also be a picture, a type of formatting, the repetition of specific ideas, and so on. The teacher would also remind students that after they create their items, they are to create another version of their items and discuss whether the second version is easier or harder than the first. They should also be able to explain why a particular change made the item easier or harder. Based on the teacher's directions, one student might produce the item in figure 3.6.

> Jana's heart was beating fast as she stepped onto the stage, and her hands were trembling. But as she played the first notes of her song on the violin, her fear melted away, and she felt herself starting to enjoy the fact that she was performing in front of people.
>
> How does the author's use of the phrase "fear melted away" help the reader understand Jana's experience as a performer?
> a. The phrase tells the reader that Jana has practiced for a long time.
> b. The phrase shows the reader that Jana was nervous before she started performing.
> c. The phrase shows that Jana was confident she would perform well.
> d. The phrase indicates that Jana no longer likes to perform.

FIGURE 3.6: Student-generated function item.

The student explains that the correct answer is option *b*: "The phrase shows the reader that Jana was nervous before she started performing." If her fear melted away, she must have been nervous before she started performing.

The student also presents a second version of the item. In this case, the student uses the same question but makes a change to the options provided for the correct answer.

a. *The phrase tells the reader that Jana has practiced for a long time.*

b. *The phrase shows the reader that Jana was nervous before she started performing.*

c. *The phrase shows that Jana enjoyed performing in front of people once she got over her fear.*

d. *The phrase indicates that Jana no longer likes to perform.*

In this list, option *c* has been changed and now reads, "The phrase shows that Jana enjoyed performing in front of people once she got over her fear." The student explains that this change makes the item harder to answer because option *c* now seems like it could be a viable answer to the question. The student explains that items like this become much harder to answer when there is more than one option that seems like the possible answer.

SUMMARY

This chapter addressed three specific steps for using item frames in the ELA classroom. Step 1 involves directly teaching the ELA content necessary to correctly answer various types of items. Step 2 involves presenting students with potential strategies for approaching the various types of item frames. Step 3 involves providing students with multiple opportunities to analyze items. These three steps might seem simple on the surface, but when executed precisely and consistently, they accomplish the task of teaching students to think the way tests make them. The same steps apply to every subject area. In the next two chapters, we consider mathematics instruction.

CHAPTER 4

CONNECTING MATHEMATICS ITEM FRAMES TO ACADEMIC CONTENT

To effectively teach students about the types of thinking required to answer mathematics items, teachers must first be aware of the types of items found on external assessments. As with ELA items, *Ethical Test Preparation in the Classroom* (Marzano, Dodson, et al., 2022) summarized the findings from an analysis of 2,629 mathematics items. Major topics were identified in grades 3 through 8. Because of the variety of secondary course progressions across schools and districts, items at the high school level were placed together in one large group. Items from the SAT and ACT were analyzed separately due to differences in the design and use of those tests.

Like ELA, a large portion of the mathematics items consisted of two or more parts. Unlike ELA, the multiple parts of mathematics items typically asked questions that were significantly distinct from one another. Whereas the second part of an ELA item might ask students to explain or support their answers to the first part, the second part of a mathematics item often asks students to perform new calculations using the same mathematical content as the original item but requires them to use different operations or different representations. Also, in contrast to the ELA analysis, the mathematics items displayed extreme diversity in terms of item format. This led the researchers to categorize mathematics items primarily by content rather than form. They identified the nine broad content categories depicted in table 4.1 (page 46).

Each of the major categories in table 4.1 (page 46) has a number of subcategories. The researchers identified every subcategory that accounted for at least 2 percent of the items on a test at a given grade level. The results of this analysis generated the topics depicted in table 4.2 (page 46).

TABLE 4.1: General Mathematics Topical Categories

CONTENT CATEGORY	NUMBER OF ITEMS	PERCENTAGE OF TOTAL ITEMS
Expressions, Equations, Inequalities, and Functions (EEIF)	676	25.71
Operations	620	23.58
Geometry	528	20.08
Quantity and Number	386	14.68
Ratios and Proportional Relationships	170	6.47
Data Displays	88	3.35
Statistics	83	3.16
Measurement	49	1.86
Trigonometry	29	1.10
Total	2,629	

Note: Percentages do not sum to 100 due to rounding.

Source: Marzano, Dodson, et al., 2022, p. 86.

TABLE 4.2: Critical Mathematics Topics by Grade Level

GRADE LEVEL	TOPICS	
Grade 3	Bar Graph Two-Way Table Expressions 2-D and 3-D Shapes Area and Perimeter Time Tools	Addition Multiplication Operation Not Specified Comparison Equivalence Fractions Number Lines
Grade 4	2-D and 3-D Shapes Area and Perimeter Lines and Angles Addition Division Multiples and Factors	Multiplication Subtraction Operation Not Specified Comparison Equivalence Place Value
Grade 5	Expressions Volume Area and Perimeter 2-D and 3-D Shapes Operation Not Specified Multiplication	Addition Division Coordinate Plane Equivalence Place Value Comparison

Grade 6	Equations Expressions Area and Perimeter Volume Division Operation Not Specified	Coordinate Plane Equivalence Percentages Rate and Ratio Number Patterns Measures of Center and Variance
Grade 7	Equations Expressions Inequalities 2-D and 3-D Shapes Area and Perimeter Operation Not Specified Coordinate Plane Equivalence	Percentages Proportional Relationships Rate and Ratio Scaling Measures of Center and Variance Probability Statistical Investigation
Grade 8	Scatterplot Equations Functions Expressions Transformations Volume Lines and Angles	Triangles Operation Not Specified Exponents, Radicals, and Scientific Notation Equivalence Rate and Ratio
High School	Functions Equations Inequalities Expressions Triangles Lines and Angles Transformations	Circles Volume 2-D and 3-D Shapes Operation Not Specified Equivalence Rate and Ratio Trigonometry

Source: Adapted from Marzano, Dodson, et al., 2022.

As is the case with ELA, the various item types within these mathematics topics should be integrated with local mathematics standards, curriculum, common assessments, or proficiency scales.

MATCHING ITEM FRAMES TO MATHEMATICS STANDARDS

The various mathematics item frames are easily matched to standards. To illustrate, consider the third-grade mathematics standards from the state of Colorado (Colorado Academic Standards, 2019a):

3.G.A. Geometry: Reason with shapes and their attributes.
   a. Explain that shapes in different categories (e.g., rhombuses, rectangles, and others) may share attributes (e.g., having four sides), and that the shared attributes can define a larger category (e.g., quadrilaterals). Recognize rhombuses, rectangles, and squares as examples of quadrilaterals, and draw examples of quadrilaterals that do not belong to any of these subcategories. (CCSS: 3.G.A.1)

This standard refers to an understanding of different categories of two-dimensional shapes and the various types of shapes in those categories. Not surprisingly, the study reported in *Ethical Test Preparation in the Classroom* (Marzano, Dodson, et al., 2022) identified items that address two-dimensional shapes as an important focus at that grade level. To illustrate, consider the item in figure 4.1.

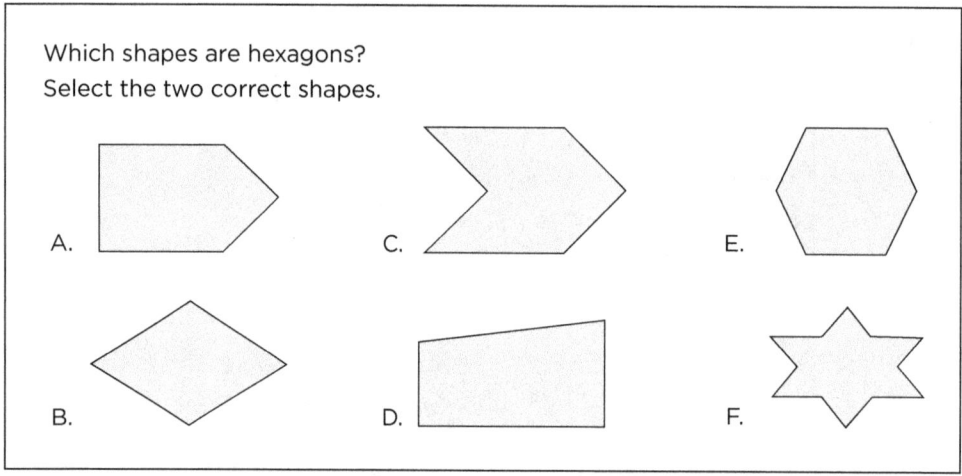

Source: Marzano, Dodson, et al., 2022, p. 193.
FIGURE 4.1: Third-grade categories of two-dimensional shapes.

In this item, students are presented with a number of two-dimensional shapes and asked to identify those that are hexagons. To reinforce the Colorado standard, teachers might generate similar items as a way to emphasize the importance of knowing the various categories of two-dimensional shapes. To this end, *Ethical Test Preparation in the Classroom* (Marzano, Dodson, et al., 2022) provided step-by-step directions on how such items can be generated. These directions are depicted in figure 4.2.

As exemplified by figure 4.2, the directions for developing mathematics items are much more abstract than those for creating ELA items. The directions for each item start with a template that represents the basic format of the item, with elements stated in abstract form. For example, *category 1* stands for the category of geometric shapes students will be looking for in the item. Item directions also include directions

Connecting Mathematics Item Frames to Academic Content 49

Template

Which shapes are [Category 1]?

Select the [Quantity 1] correct shapes.

   a. [Shape 1]   d. [Shape 4]

   b. [Shape 2]   e. [Shape 5]

   c. [Shape 3]   f. [Shape 6]

Instructions

1. Define [Category 1] according to the specifications in the key. Insert this definition into the template.
2. Select [Quantity 1] according to the specifications in the key. Insert this quantity into the template.
3. Use the Shapes tool under the Insert tab to draw [Shapes 1–6] according to the specifications in the key.

Key

Category 1: A category of two-dimensional shapes (for example, quadrilaterals, triangles, hexagons)

Quantity 1: A whole-number quantity from 2–5

Shapes 1–6: Various two-dimensional shapes, [Quantity 1] of which belong to [Category 1]

Source: Adapted from Marzano, Dodson, et al., 2022.

FIGURE 4.2: Directions for constructing two-dimensional shape items.

about how to use the abstract elements. For example, the directions in figure 4.2 indicate that the teacher should define category 1 according to the specifications in the key and then insert the definition into the template. Finally, item directions have a key that provides the specification of each abstract element. For example, the key defines category 1 as "a category of two-dimensional shapes (for example, quadrilaterals, triangles, hexagons)."

The directions for each item type are detailed enough that teachers can design their own items that mimic the item frames identified in the comprehensive study of mathematics tests.

MATCHING ITEM FRAMES TO THE CURRICULUM

Another way to use mathematics item frames is to match them to specific parts of the curriculum. This can be accomplished by examining the contents of a specific textbook or program in the school. For example, a middle school that is using a specific mathematics textbook might examine the various modules into which the series is organized. One of the modules at the middle school level addresses the mathematics topic of rates. Scanning the list of item types in *Ethical Test Preparation in the*

Classroom (Marzano, Dodson, et al., 2022), teachers conclude that there are specific item frames for this aspect of mathematics they would like to use in their classes. A sample item for this topic is depicted in figure 4.3.

A farmer's field produces 1,008 bushels of corn from 9 acres.
Fill in the number of bushels the field produces from 20 acres at this rate.

[   ]

FIGURE 4.3: Rate problem.

The directions for creating new items for this topic are depicted in figure 4.4. Using these directions, teachers can create multiple versions of the item and embed them as practice items when teaching the content from the textbook.

Template
[Person] [Activity] [Quantity 1] [Unit 1] [Relation] [Quantity 2] [Unit 2]
Fill in the number of [Unit 1] the [Person] [Activity] [Relation] [Quantity 3] [Unit 2] at this rate.

Instructions
1. Choose definitions for [Person], [Activity], and [Relation] and insert them into the template.
2. Select the first unit by which [Activity] is measured and insert it into the template as [Unit 1].
3. Select the unit relative to which [Unit 1] is measured in [Activity] and insert it into the template as [Unit 2].
4. Select a unit rate of [Unit 1] per [Unit 2]. This unit rate may be a decimal if desired.
5. Select the number of units of [Unit 2] for the initial rate presented in the problem according to the specifications in the key and insert it into the template as [Quantity 2].
6. Multiply the unit rate from step 4 by [Quantity 2] and insert the product into the template as [Quantity 1].
7. Select the number of units of [Unit 2] for the second rate presented in the problem according to the specifications in the key and insert it into the template as [Quantity 3].

Key
Person: Any person or entity (for example, a plane, a farmer's field, a pool)
Activity: Any activity that can be measured by two different units in a rate relationship (for example, traveling, producing corn, being filled)
Relation: Any word or phrase relating the first entity in the rate relationship with the second (for example, *in, from, over*)

Connecting Mathematics Item Frames to Academic Content 51

> Unit 1: Any measurement unit in which the first entity of the rate relationship is measured (for example, miles, bushels, gallons)
>
> Unit 2: Any measurement unit in which the first entity of the rate relationship is measured (for example, minutes, acres, seconds)
>
> Quantity 1: Any whole number greater than 1
>
> Quantity 2: Any whole number greater than 1. Care should be taken that the product of [Quantity 2] and the unit rate from step 4 of the instructions (that is, [Quantity 2] × Unit Rate) is a whole number.
>
> Quantity 3: Any whole number greater than [Quantity 2]. Care should be taken that the product of [Quantity 3] and the unit rate from step 4 of the instructions (that is, [Quantity 3] × Unit Rate) is a whole number.

Source: Adapted from Marzano, Dodson, et al., 2022.
FIGURE 4.4: Directions for creating rate problems.

One of the more powerful aspects of the instructions for developing items is that they commonly provide insight into the complexity of seemingly simple items. For example, the item about the farmer's field producing bushels of corn can be stated in a couple sentences. However, the instructions disclose the fact that this item involves a number of mathematical elements interacting in complex ways.

MATCHING ITEM FRAMES TO COMMON ASSESSMENTS

As described in chapter 2 (page 17), item frames fit well in common assessments developed by collaborative teams. For example, assume a collaborative team of fifth-grade mathematics teachers decides it wants to construct a common assessment regarding the topic of volume. Since the team has identified the topic that will be the focus of its common assessment, the team members now look for item frames associated with the topic of volume. Consulting *Ethical Test Preparation in the Classroom* (Marzano, Dodson, et al., 2022), the team finds a fifth-grade item frame like the one in figure 4.5 (page 52).

The collaborative team members note that in their classes, they do cover the topic of volume of right rectangular prisms but do not expose students to the convention at the end of part A of the item. In other words, they do ask students to generate equations for determining the volume of such prisms, but they do not force students to select which numbers in a specific list are part of these equations. They conclude that this requirement has nothing to do with the ability to compute the volume of such figures, but they feel they must design the items on the common assessment to include such restrictions to make students aware of this rather odd convention in test design. The collaborative team members decide that this convention should be

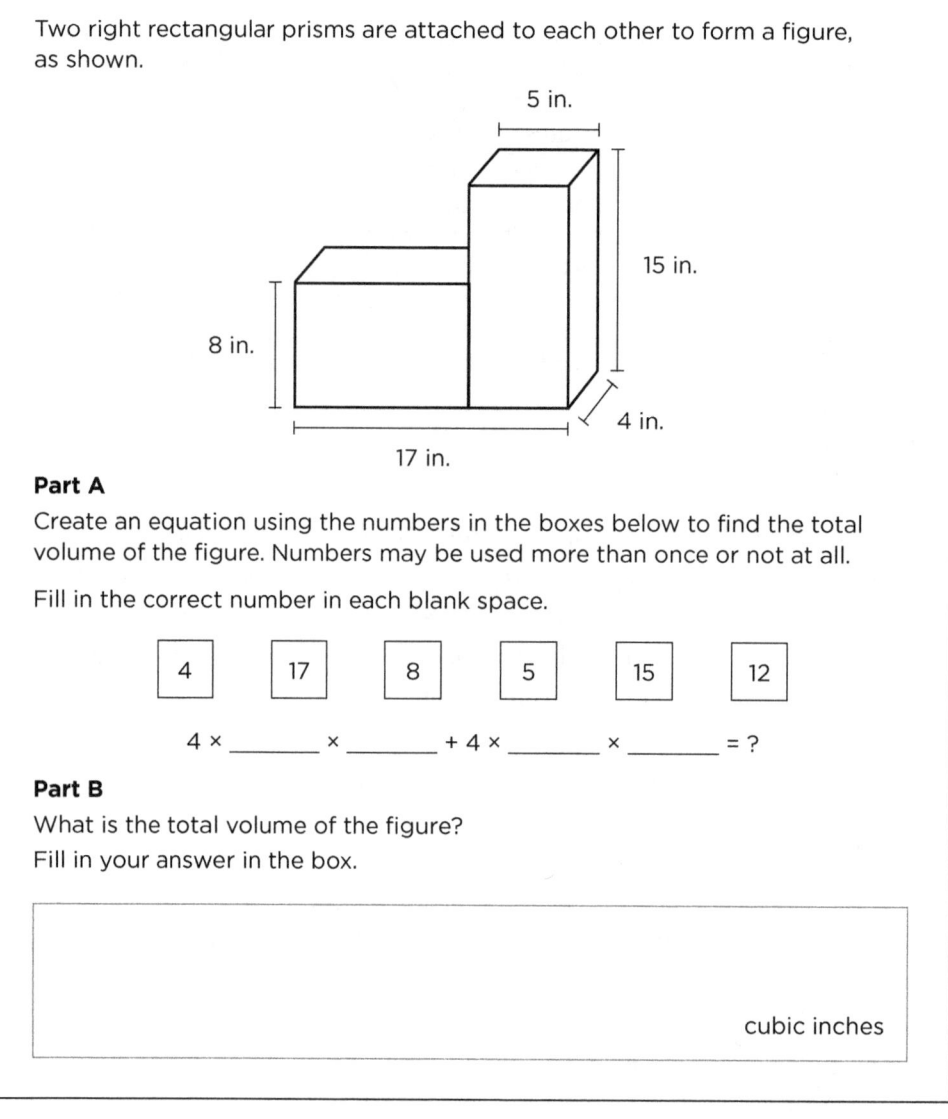

FIGURE 4.5: Fifth-grade mathematics item on volume.

something they directly teach students. In effect, this awareness should become part of students' schema for this particular type of item.

MATCHING ITEM FRAMES TO PROFICIENCY SCALES

As described previously, proficiency scales are statements of knowledge and skill for specific topics organized into a continuum of knowledge. For example, figure 4.6 displays a proficiency scale for the middle school topic of rate.

4.0	The student: • Demonstrates inferences and applications that go beyond what was directly taught
3.5	In addition to score 3.0 performance, partial success at score 4.0 content
3.0	The student can calculate rates to solve problems involving equivalent ratios (for example, when given the problem, "A family completed a road trip of 195 miles in 3 hours driving at a constant speed. Determine how long it would have taken them to complete a trip of 325 miles driving at the same speed"). The student exhibits no major errors or omissions relative to this content.
2.5	No major errors or omissions regarding score 2.0 content, and partial success at score 3.0 content
2.0	The student demonstrates an understanding of and ability to execute basic processes such as: • The rate of a given ratio can be calculated by dividing the first quantity of the ratio by the second quantity. For example, when given the ratio "15 apples to 10 oranges," the rate of apples to oranges can be calculated as: $$(15 \div 10) \text{ apples per orange} = \frac{3}{2} \text{ apples per orange}$$ • Two or more ratios can be compared by calculating and comparing their rates. For example, when given the ratio of boys to girls in each sixth-grade class in a school, the classes that have the highest and lowest ratios of boys to girls can be identified by calculating the rate of boys per girl for each class and then comparing the rates. • A set of equivalent ratios can be used as a set of value pairs in which the values of each pair are related to each other by a multiplier that is constant across all pairs. For example, when given the set of equivalent ratios $x_1:y_1$ and $x_2:y_2$, the values of each pair are related to each other by a constant multiplier k, such that $x_1 \times k = y_1$ and $x_2 \times k = y_2$. • Multiplicative comparisons and additive comparisons are different when testing for ratio equivalence. For example, when given the pairs of related values (x_1, y_1), (x_2, y_2), (x_3, y_3), the ratio equivalence is indicated by the fact that each y value is related to its corresponding x value by a constant multiplier ($\frac{y_1}{x_1} = \frac{y_2}{x_2} = \frac{y_3}{x_3}$) rather than by any equivalence in the difference between corresponding or consecutive values ($y_1 - x_1 = y_2 - x_2 = y_3 - x_3$ or $y_3 - y_2 = y_2 - y_1$). • There are situations in which ratios will be equivalent (will have the same rate). For example, the rate of millimeters to inches will be constant for all length measurements.
1.5	Partial success at score 2.0 content, and major errors or omissions regarding score 3.0 content
1.0	With help, partial success at score 2.0 content and score 3.0 content
0.5	With help, partial success at score 2.0 content but not at score 3.0 content
0.0	Even with help, no success

Source: © 2016 by Marzano Resources. Adapted with permission.
FIGURE 4.6: Mathematics proficiency scale.

As was described in chapter 2 (page 17) regarding ELA frames, teachers can identify item frames that would fulfill the requirements of score 3.0 of the proficiency scale. In this case, a teacher might create items like those shown in figure 4.7.

> A delivery truck travels 240 miles in 4 hours at a constant speed.
> **Part A:** What is the speed of the truck in miles per hour?
> **Part B:** At the same speed, how long would it take the truck to travel 420 miles?
> **Part C:** How far can the truck travel in 7 hours?
>
> A water pump fills 75 gallons of water in 15 minutes at a constant rate.
> **Part A:** What is the pump's filling rate in gallons per minute?
> **Part B:** How many gallons of water can the pump fill in 1 hour?
> **Part C:** How long will it take the pump to fill a tank with a capacity of 300 gallons?

FIGURE 4.7: Sample items for rates and ratios.

INTEGRATING ITEM FRAMES INTO PROFICIENCY SCALES

Also as described in the discussion of ELA proficiency scales, item frames can be embedded in proficiency scales to create more specific 3.0 score values. Again, this makes score 3.0 of the proficiency scale similar to instructional objectives as described by Mager (1962). Also, score 4.0 of the scale includes the expectation that students can design their own items, alter such items, and explain the impact of their changes on the item's difficulty. A sample scale with an item embedded is depicted in figure 4.8.

4.0	The student can: • Modify the frame to make it easier, and explain why the modification works • Modify the frame to make it more difficult, and explain why the modification works
3.5	In addition to score 3.0 performance, partial success at score 4.0 content
3.0	The student can calculate rates to solve problems involving equivalent ratios, especially in problems like the following. • A family completed a road trip of 195 miles in 3 hours driving at a constant speed. Determine how long it would have taken them to complete a trip of 325 miles driving at the same speed. The student directly answers such items independently.

	Additionally, the student can describe a reasonable strategy for addressing items of this type. Such a strategy might be a unique creation of the student's, or it might contain information presented to the student about: • The content important for item success • The item type
2.5	No major errors or omissions regarding score 2.0 content, and partial success at score 3.0 content
2.0	The student understands the content elements necessary for item success. Specifically, the student knows that: • The rate of a given ratio can be calculated by dividing the first quantity of the ratio by the second quantity. For example, when given the ratio "15 apples to 10 oranges," the rate of apples to oranges can be calculated as: $(15 \div 10)$ apples per orange $= \frac{3}{2}$ apples per orange • Two or more ratios can be compared by calculating and comparing their rates. For example, when given the ratio of boys to girls in each sixth-grade class in a school, the classes that have the highest and lowest ratios of boys to girls can be identified by calculating the rate of boys per girl for each class and then comparing the rates. • A set of equivalent ratios can be used as a set of value pairs in which the values of each pair are related to each other by a multiplier that is constant across all pairs. For example, when given the set of equivalent ratios $x_1:y_1$ and $x_2:y_2$, the values of each pair are related to each other by a constant multiplier k, such that $x_1 \times k = y_1$ and $x_2 \times k = y_2$. • Multiplicative comparisons and additive comparisons are different when testing for ratio equivalence. For example, when given the pairs of related values (x_1, y_1), (x_2, y_2), (x_3, y_3), the ratio equivalence is indicated by the fact that each y value is related to its corresponding x value by a constant multiplier ($\frac{y_1}{x_1} = \frac{y_2}{x_2} = \frac{y_3}{x_3}$) rather than by any equivalence in the difference between corresponding or consecutive values ($y_1 - x_1 = y_2 - x_2 = y_3 - x_3$ or $y_3 - y_2 = y_2 - y_1$). • There are situations in which ratios will be equivalent (will have the same rate). For example, the rate of millimeters to inches will be constant for all length measurements.
1.5	Partial success at score 2.0 content, and major errors or omissions regarding score 3.0 content
1.0	With help, partial success at score 2.0 content and score 3.0 content
0.5	With help, partial success at score 2.0 content but not at score 3.0 content
0.0	Even with help, no success

FIGURE 4.8: Proficiency scale with embedded item.

Finally, the score 2.0 content in the proficiency scale would be the focus of direct instruction in class. In this case, that content is as follows.

- The rate of a given ratio can be calculated by dividing the first quantity of the ratio by the second quantity. For example, when given the ratio "15 apples to 10 oranges," the rate of apples to oranges can be calculated as:
  - (15 ÷ 10) apples per orange = 3/2 apples per orange
- Two or more ratios can be compared by calculating and comparing their rates. For example, when given the ratio of boys to girls in each sixth-grade class in a school, the classes that have the highest and lowest ratios of boys to girls can be identified by calculating the rate of boys per girl for each class and then comparing the rates.
- A set of equivalent ratios can be used as a set of value pairs in which the values of each pair are related to each other by a multiplier that is constant across all pairs. For example, when given the set of equivalent ratios $x_1:y_1$ and $x_2:y_2$, the values of each pair are related to each other by a constant multiplier k, such that $x_1 \times k = y_1$ and $x_2 \times k = y_2$.
- Multiplicative comparisons and additive comparisons are different when testing for ratio equivalence. For example, when given the pairs of related values (x_1, y_1), (x_2, y_2), (x_3, y_3), the ratio equivalence is indicated by the fact that each y value is related to its corresponding x value by a constant multiplier ($y_1/x_1 = y_2/x_2 = y_3/x_3$) rather than by any equivalence in the difference between corresponding or consecutive values ($y_1 - x_1 = y_2 - x_2 = y_3 - x_3$ or $y_3 - y_2 = y_2 - y_1$).
- There are situations in which ratios will be equivalent (will have the same rate). For example, the rate of millimeters to inches will be constant for all length measurements.

SUMMARY

This chapter described the study of 2,629 mathematics test items on state, national, and international tests reported in *Ethical Test Preparation in the Classroom* (Marzano, Dodson, et al., 2022), which found significant differences in the mathematics topics addressed from grade level to grade level. This chapter focused on four different ways these item frames can be integrated into regular classroom instruction: (1) matching item frames to standards, (2) matching item frames to the curriculum, (3) matching item frames to common assessments, and (4) matching item frames to proficiency scales. Due to the nature of mathematics content, the directions for teachers to create their own items are abstract and complex. This chapter laid the basic groundwork for teachers to understand the nature of the mathematics item frames found on many large-scale assessments. With this foundational knowledge, teachers should be prepared to use the strategies presented in the next chapter.

CHAPTER 5

USING MATHEMATICS ITEM FRAMES IN CLASSROOM INSTRUCTION

With mathematics item frames matched with state standards, the mathematics curriculum, common assessments, or proficiency scales, teachers should have clear guidance as to which item frames to use in specific situations. They should also be provided with guidance as to how they might use mathematics item frames in the classroom. The three steps to this process (which are the same as those for ELA; see chapter 3, page 35) are described in the following sections.

STEP 1: TEACH THE CONTENT THAT IS THE FOCUS OF THE ITEM FRAME

The obvious first step when using mathematics item frames is to teach the content the item is designed to assess. Ideally, this content is in a proficiency scale the school has created with a specific item frame in mind. To illustrate, consider the proficiency scale in figure 5.1 (page 58), which focuses on the topic of equivalent expressions at the sixth-grade level.

The score 2.0 elements in the proficiency scale represent the information students must know to navigate the mathematics content the item is designed to assess. In this case, that content includes information about equivalent expressions and the various operations that can be performed on them. Such information includes the following.

- Expressions can look different but still be equivalent. One way to tell if one expression is equal to another is to simplify both expressions as much as possible. For example, an expression such as $4(5x + 2y)$ can be simplified to $20x + 8y$. If you still are not sure once the expressions have

4.0	The student can: • Modify the frame to make it easier, and explain why the modification works • Modify the frame to make it more difficult, and explain why the modification works
3.5	In addition to score 3.0 performance, partial success at score 4.0 content
3.0	The student can analyze and create equivalent expressions to represent various mathematical quantities, as depicted in problems like the following. Select all of the expressions that are equivalent to $3(7x + 5y)$. • $21x + 5y$ • $3(7x) + 3(5y)$ • $21x + 15y$ • $3(12xy)$ • $10x + 8y$ The student can perform such tasks independently. Additionally, the student can describe a reasonable strategy for addressing items of this type. Such a strategy might be a unique creation of the student's, or it might contain information presented to the student about: • The content important for item success • The item type
2.5	No major errors or omissions regarding score 2.0 content, and partial success at score 3.0 content
2.0	The student understands the content elements necessary for item success. Specifically, the student knows that: • Expressions can look different but still be equivalent. One way to tell if one expression is equal to another is to simplify both expressions as much as possible. For example, an expression such as $4(5x + 2y)$ can be simplified to $20x + 8y$. If you still are not sure once the expressions have been simplified, you can set one expression equal to the other. All whole numbers and variables will cancel out in expressions that are equivalent. • Another way to tell whether two expressions are equivalent is to substitute values for variables and solve the equation. Equivalent expressions will have the same answer. • The order of operations is parentheses, exponents, multiplication/division, addition/subtraction.
1.5	Partial success at score 2.0 content, and major errors or omissions regarding score 3.0 content
1.0	With help, partial success at score 2.0 content and score 3.0 content
0.5	With help, partial success at score 2.0 content but not at score 3.0 content
0.0	Even with help, no success

FIGURE 5.1: Sixth-grade mathematics proficiency scale with item-embedded item frame.

been simplified, you can set one expression equal to the other. All whole numbers and variables will cancel out in expressions that are equivalent.

- Another way to tell whether two expressions are equivalent is to substitute values for variables and solve the equation. Equivalent expressions will have the same answer.
- The order of operations is parentheses, exponents, multiplication/division, addition/subtraction.

This type of content should be directly taught to and exemplified for students. It is useful to start instruction with a pretest or a quick survey of the content, like the one depicted in figure 5.2.

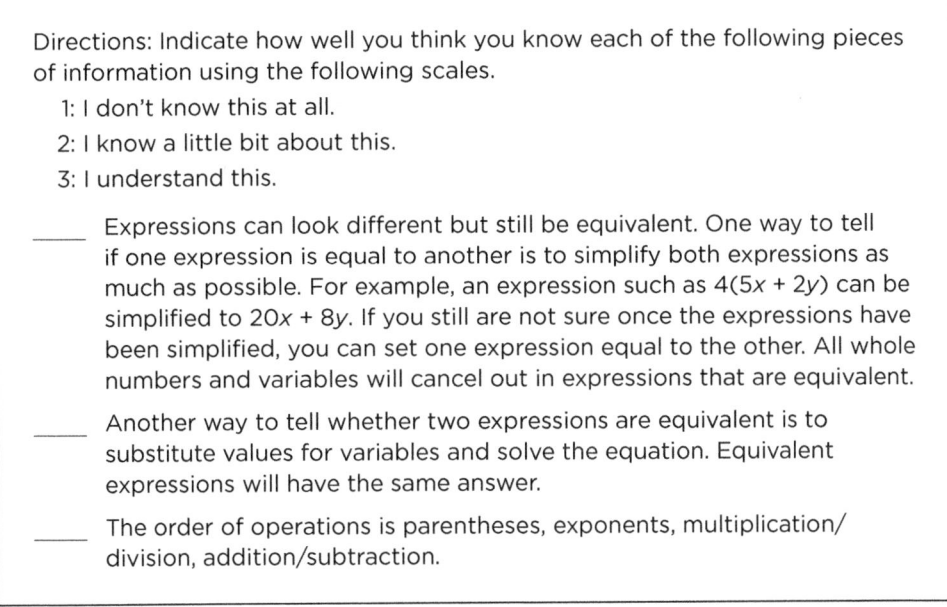

FIGURE 5.2: Student survey of mathematics content.

If the teacher sees gaps in students' knowledge, then they intervene with direct instruction. For example, assume a student survey indicated a lack of knowledge in the first element at score 2.0 of the proficiency scale, which deals with equivalent expressions that look different (see figure 5.1). Based on this information about students' needs, the teacher would plan a set of lessons specifically designed to teach and reinforce this content, paying particular attention to providing students with adequate practice in simplifying expressions to determine equivalence.

STEP 2: PRESENT STUDENTS WITH POTENTIAL STRATEGIES FOR APPROACHING THE ITEM

This step directly addresses the score 3.0 content in the proficiency scale that deals with strategies for addressing specific types of items. Recall that at score 3.0, students are expected to describe a reasonable strategy for addressing items of this type. Such a strategy might be a unique creation of the student's, or it might contain information presented to the student about:

- The content important for item success
- The item type

The strategies students create should focus directly on the specific problem type articulated at score 3.0. In this case, that problem type is shown in figure 5.3.

The student can analyze and create equivalent expressions to represent various mathematical quantities, as depicted in problems like the following. Select all of the expressions that are equivalent to $3(7x + 5y)$.

☐ $21x + 5y$
☐ $3(7x) + 3(5y)$
☐ $21x + 15y$
☐ $3(12xy)$
☐ $10x + 8y$

FIGURE 5.3: Sixth-grade equivalent expressions problem.

To help students develop their own approaches to these types of items, the teacher should present them with a variety of possible strategies and information with which to create strategies, such as the following.

- This type of item asks you to identify one or more expressions that are equivalent to a given expression. The expression may have up to two variables. You are not being asked to solve the expression.
- To find equivalent expressions, use what you know about the order of operations to determine if the expression can be further altered. For example, $4(5x + 2y)$ is an expression that has a multiplication operation hiding inside of it. If you execute that multiplication operation, you have $20x + 8y$.
- If your expression is already broken down into individual parts, you can reverse the process and think backward about what numbers and operations are hiding within each part. For example, if you have an equation like $12x + 6y$, then you also have one like $6(2x + y)$. You may also have an equation like $6(x + y + x)$.

○ You can check your work by choosing values for the variables in the given expression and solving it. Your chosen equivalent expressions should also have the same solution.

The expectation here is that teachers present students with explicit strategies to address specific items. But students are not expected or encouraged to use these strategies in a mechanical or rote manner. Instead, they take what they have learned from the teacher and create their own unique strategies for addressing specific items.

STEP 3: PROVIDE STUDENTS WITH MULTIPLE OPPORTUNITIES TO ANALYZE ITEMS

On a regular basis, students should have multiple opportunities to interact with item frames that have been selected as the focus of instruction. Such interaction should go well beyond simply asking students to answer items as a form of practice. Rather, with each encounter with an item, students should be asked to analyze the item types and their thinking regarding the item types. There are a number of ways to do this, which the following sections describe.

Teacher Alterations

When using this approach, the teacher presents an item to students but then makes alterations in the item. To illustrate, first refer back to the mathematics item on equivalent expressions in figure 5.3. The teacher would first provide students with time to answer this question and then have them discuss their answers in small groups. The teacher might also lead a whole-class discussion of the item.

After the discussion, the teacher would provide students with an altered version of the item like the one in figure 5.4. The teacher has replaced the last option with another equivalent expression. Now, three of the five options are correct, as opposed to only two in the original problem. The students note that this has made the problem slightly more difficult, particularly because the new expression has larger numbers, which call for a little more factoring to get to the original version.

Select all of the expressions that are equivalent to $3(7x + 5y)$.
☐ $21x + 5y$
☐ $3(7x) + 3(5y)$
☐ $21x + 15y$
☐ $3(12xy)$
☐ $3(5x + 5y + 2x)$

FIGURE 5.4: Altered item on sixth-grade equivalent expressions.

The teacher then asks each student to summarize what they have learned about the content the item was designed to assess or the type of item itself. Students conclude that the more potentially correct alternatives there are in an item, the more complex thinking it takes to discern the correct answers.

Student Alterations

Once students become comfortable with teacher alterations, they can be asked to make their own alterations. In this situation, the teacher would present students with an item like the one in figure 5.5 and have them answer the item and then discuss their answers in small groups. This problem again relates to equivalent expressions but is a different item than previous examples.

Select all of the expressions that are equivalent to $2(4x + 6y)$.
☐ $8x + 12y$
☐ $2(4x) + 2(6y)$
☐ $20x + 12y$
☐ $2(24xy)$

FIGURE 5.5: Original item presented to students.

The teacher would ask students to change some aspect of the item and determine if the change made the item easier or harder. Students might do this independently and then share their altered item in small groups. For example, one student might create the altered equivalent expressions item in figure 5.6.

Select all of the expressions that are equivalent to $2(4x + 6y)$.
☐ $8x + 12y$
☐ $2(4x) + 2(6y)$
☐ $20x + 12y$
☐ $2(24xy)$
☐ $2(4x + 6y) - 0(xy)$

FIGURE 5.6: Student-altered sixth-grade equivalent expressions item.

The student might explain that this alteration makes the item a little more difficult than the original because it adds a mathematical concept to the problem, namely that multiplying variables by 0 adds nothing to an expression and therefore keeps the expression equivalent, even though a new term has been added.

Student-Generated Items

When students have had adequate experience with a specific item type, they can be asked to create their own items, alter their own items, and describe why their alterations made it easier or harder. Again, assume we are still dealing with an equivalent expressions item frame. Students would start by creating a unique item. A student might create the following equivalent expressions item.

Simplify the following expressions and determine if they are equivalent.

1. $2(a + 3)$
2. $2a + 6$

The teacher would then have students change their created items and describe whether the newest version is easier or harder. This particular student might change the second expression from $2a + 6$ to $10a + 30$ and explain that it is now more difficult because both expressions must be factored to get them into a form where they can't be simplified any further.

SUMMARY

This chapter addressed three specific steps that are involved in using item frames in the mathematics classroom (the same as those used with ELA items). Step 1 involves directly teaching the mathematics content necessary to correctly answer various types of items. Step 2 involves presenting students with potential strategies for approaching the various types of item frames. Step 3 involves providing students with multiple opportunities to analyze items. These three steps are designed to teach students to think the way tests make them.

CHAPTER 6

SUPPORTING AND INTEGRATING THE USE OF ITEM FRAMES

Item frame instruction does not occur in isolation. Rather, it should be integrated into other practices designed to enhance students' learning. In this chapter, we address four instructional practices that complement item frames instruction: (1) cumulative review, (2) journaling, (3) questioning techniques, and (4) guided discourse. Additionally, this chapter presents a comprehensible process that integrates all of these components, referred to as *the successive relearning instructional cycle*. Finally, this chapter presents examples of the use of test-specific thinking strategies from various subject areas and grade levels.

CUMULATIVE REVIEW

Cumulative review is a process that focuses on students' recall and analysis of content they are learning. This practice is supported by a growing body of research. As articulated in the neuroscience literature, teachers should consider the act of recalling as one of the more powerful tools in learning (Oakley, Rogowsky, & Sejnowski, 2021). That said, it is important that students don't simply recall information to working memory. After students have retrieved information, they should scrutinize that information and alter it as necessary. Cumulative review is one way teachers can achieve this goal. In the cognitive science literature, cumulative review would fit into a category of strategies referred to as *successive relearning* (Higham, Zengel, Bartlett, & Hadwin, 2022). Successive relearning is a broad term that refers to strategies involving students systematically going back to topics they have previously learned and adding to and restructuring their current knowledge base.

Cumulative review is one of the premier strategies to enhance students' recall and understanding of content (Marzano & Kosena, 2022). The cumulative-review process involves three phases: (1) record, (2) review, and (3) revise. These three phases produce the best results when executed as an integrated event.

In the first phase of cumulative review, students *record* what they remember about a topic that was previously introduced to them. This can manifest in many forms, such as summary statements, outlines, graphic representations with notes, a "brain dump" that utilizes unconnected ideas and words, and so on. Regardless of which recording structure is used, during this phase, students recall and record what they understand about a specific topic using their own words and representations.

The *review* phase of cumulative review requires students to examine or test their understanding of the content. There are various ways to complete this phase as well. For example, a teacher might ask students to answer inferential questions about the topic of focus or compare the content in the topic to the content in a related topic. Similarly, the teacher might ask students to identify the category the topic belongs to or the subcategories within the topic.

Revise is the final phase of the cumulative-review process. It is this step that helps students alter and enhance their knowledge of the topic they are reviewing. It is also the step of the cumulative-review process that is probably skipped most often. To ensure this phase is executed effectively, teachers might ask students to engage in the following steps.

1. **Examine your understanding of the topic:** Students determine how well they think they know a topic.
2. **Identify any misconceptions about the topic or related topics:** Students identify things they thought they were right about but, in fact, were not.
3. **Fill in any gaps:** Students identify missing information in their understanding and fill in such information.
4. **Add new information:** Students add new details, generalizations, and principles to their current understanding.
5. **Explain your reasoning:** Students examine how they have come to specific conclusions about the topic.

With this general understanding of cumulative review in mind, we next consider the role of item frames in the process, the connection of cumulative review to other review and note-taking strategies, and the recommended frequency of cumulative review.

The Role of Item Frames in Cumulative Review

Item frames fit well within the cumulative-review process. For example, assume that a teacher has selected the topic of understanding the important details in texts as the focus of cumulative review. In the first phase (record), students record what they remember about focusing on details while they read. Some students might record information about the types of details that are commonly important in texts that describe complex cause-and-effect relationships, such as the following.

- Who was involved in the cause-and-effect relationship
- What occurred as a result of the cause-and-effect relationship
- Where the cause-and-effect relationship occurred
- When the cause-and-effect relationship occurred
- Why the cause-and-effect relationship occurred
- How the cause-and-effect relationship occurred

Other students might record information about the types of details that are commonly important in texts that describe plots with multiple storylines.

- Who was involved in various phases of the plot
- What occurred during various phases of the plot
- Where various phases of the plot occurred
- When various phases of the plot occurred
- Why various phases of the plot occurred
- How various phases of the plot occurred

During the second phase (review), the teacher would introduce an item frame. To illustrate, assume a teacher presented students with the item in figure 6.1 (page 68). The teacher would present this item to students and provide time for them to answer it. The teacher might then have students discuss their answers in groups. Given that the focus of this cumulative-review process is to help students better understand the concept that details are an important tool authors use to relay information, the passage selected should be rich in detail, as is the case in figure 6.1 (page 68).

Next, the teacher would engage students in one of the activities mentioned in chapter 3 (page 35) to provide them with ways to interact with and analyze item frames. The teacher might:

- Make a change in the item and ask students to explain why the item is easier or harder
- Have students change some aspect of the item and discuss how and why the change made the item easier or harder
- Have students generate their own version of the item and then make a change in their item and explain why it is now easier or harder

In effect, activities regarding an item frame can be used during the review phase of cumulative review to ensure that students delve deeply into the content.

> **"The Wolf in Sheep's Clothing"**
>
> A certain Wolf could not get enough to eat because of the watchfulness of the Shepherds (1). But one night he found a sheep skin that had been cast aside and forgotten (2). The next day, dressed in the skin, the Wolf strolled into the pasture with the Sheep (3). Soon a little Lamb was following him about and was quickly led away to slaughter (4).
>
> That evening the Wolf entered the fold with the flock (5). But it happened that the Shepherd took a fancy for mutton broth that very evening, and, picking up a knife, went to the fold (6). There the first he laid hands on and killed was the Wolf (7).
>
> **Part A**
>
> Based on the text, how is the Wolf able to get into the pasture with the Sheep?
>   a. The Shepherds do not watch the Sheep very carefully.
>   b. A Lamb begins to follow the Wolf around.
>   c. The Wolf eats a Lamb.
>   d. The Wolf dresses itself in a sheepskin.
>
> **Part B**
>
> What information in the story best supports the answer to part A?
>   a. Sentence 1
>   b. Sentence 3
>   c. Sentence 4
>   d. Sentence 7

Source for passage: Æsop, n.d.

FIGURE 6.1: Item inserted into the review phase of cumulative review.

During phase three of cumulative review (revise), students revise their thinking regarding the topic that was the focus of the cumulative-review process. Some students might note that they had not realized before that details commonly carry some of the most important information in a text. Or some students might conclude that they must consciously pay more attention to details in the texts they read.

Cumulative Review and Related Strategies

In addition to its simple integration with item frames, cumulative review is also compatible with other common approaches to taking notes and interacting with information. Educators who see a strong connection between cumulative review and another recording or reviewing process can either embed aspects of cumulative review into that process or embed elements of the other process into cumulative review. It is perfectly legitimate for educators to blend practices they find useful.

As one example, AVID (Advancement Via Individual Determination), a schoolwide system that aims to improve learning and performance from elementary through postsecondary levels, offers a number of study-skills strategies for online and hybrid learning, including one variation referred to as the *10-2-2 model* (AVID Open Access, n.d.). It can be described as follows.

1. **Break up information:** Break the information into chunks. This could include information from reading, listening to a lecture, watching a video, or working in groups.
2. **Take notes:** Take notes for ten minutes (record phase in cumulative review).
3. **Process notes:** Spend two minutes processing the notes. This could include highlighting, circling, chunking, questioning, adding, or deleting (review phase in cumulative review).
4. **Collaborate:** Spend two minutes collaborating with a partner on the notes. This could include revising, adding to, deleting, or questioning (review phase in cumulative review).
5. **Reflect:** Spend two minutes reflecting on and revising the notes individually (revise phase in cumulative review).
6. **Repeat:** Repeat the process after each ten minutes of new content.

Although there is not a one-to-one match between the two processes, the general flow of thinking and interactions with the content in the 10-2-2 process is quite similar to that in the cumulative-review process.

Step 1 in the 10-2-2 process is not directly related to cumulative review but is related to an important instructional approach called *chunking content* (Marzano, 2017; Marzano & Abbott, 2022), which means "to present new content in short, digestible bites" (that is, *chunks*; Marzano & Abbott, 2022, p. 41) to make it manageable for students to process. Step 2 in the 10-2-2 process is directly related to the first phase of cumulative review, in which students record what they understand or recall about the particular topic that is the focus of review. Steps 3 and 4 of 10-2-2 are analogous to the review phase of cumulative review, in which students filter through the content they have recorded, making critical judgments about the nature of the content and their understanding of it. Step 5 of 10-2-2 is akin to the revise phase of cumulative review, where students articulate and record alterations in their thinking about a topic based on the analysis generated in the first two phases. Finally, step 6 is what most separates 10-2-2 from cumulative review: 10-2-2 is a very short-cycle process in that it occurs after every chunk of information. As described in the next section, cumulative review is a long-cycle process occurring ideally every week.

Frequency of Cumulative Review

Ideally, cumulative review should occur once per week. While it can be less frequent than this, we have found that once per week seems to solidify the process in students' minds as a regular and expected part of instruction.

Every week, the teacher selects a topic of focus for the three phases. This is more efficient and effective if teachers identify the topics they will address over the course of the school year, and even more so if a whole school or district identifies the topics to be covered so they are consistent across grade levels and subject areas. For example, the school or district might identify the following topics for fifth-grade mathematics to be covered throughout the school year.

1. Standard algorithm multiplication
2. Dividing multidigit numbers
3. Solving problems with place values
4. Solving fraction addition and subtraction equations
5. Fraction multiplication with models
6. Interpreting multiplication by fractions
7. Representing quotients as fractions
8. Dividing whole numbers by unit fractions
9. Manipulating decimal place values
10. Addition and subtraction of decimal values
11. Multiplication and division of decimal values
12. Whole-number exponents
13. Evaluating powers of 10
14. Numerical expressions
15. Numerical pattern relationships on a coordinate plane
16. Metric and U.S. customary units of measurement
17. Volume of rectangular prisms and solids
18. Two-dimensional figures
19. Graphing points on coordinate planes

We refer to such lists as *measurement topics* because students are assessed and scored (that is, measured) on each one. As described in previous chapters, each of these topics would have an accompanying proficiency scale. As teachers move through these topics over the course of the school year, they would focus on one previously learned topic for the cumulative-review process each week. In doing so, the teacher helps students link the current topics being reviewed and previous topics that have been reviewed.

JOURNALING

When people hear the term *journaling*, they commonly think of reflectively recording one's thoughts and its benefits, as evidenced by the journals of great historical figures such as Anne Frank, Nelson Mandela, and Leonardo da Vinci. Here, we refer to the process of journaling for the purposes of recording and updating one's thinking over time.

The recognition that writing is a powerful tool for learning dates back to the 1960s and 1970s when educators in English began using writing for the express purposes of recording and developing one's thinking relative to a specific academic topic. This became known as *writing about* academic content (Graham, Kiuhara, & MacKay, 2020). A number of meta-analyses have demonstrated that writing about academic content does indeed enhance students' learning across a wide spectrum of subject areas (Bangert-Drowns, Hurley, & Wilkinson, 2004; Graham et al., 2020; Graham & Perin, 2007). In the context of this book's recommendations, journaling focuses on improving students' knowledge of the content and deepening their understanding of the learning process itself. In the research literature, such a process is commonly referred to as *writing to learn* (Marzano, Dodson, et al., 2022).

One of the more interesting things about the writing process is that, by its very nature, it is a creative act. When students write about content, they forge connections they did not know they had. Researcher and theorist James Britton galvanized this perspective in the 1980s. As noted by Steve Graham, Sharlene A. Kiuhara, and Meade MacKay (2020):

> [Britton] claimed that writers do not know exactly what they will say when they begin to convert an idea into written text, and that the semantics and syntax of language shape this process, resulting in new learning about an idea at the "point of utterance." (p. 181)

In other words, writing helps us discover, connect, and deepen our knowledge. It also improves our communication practices. It is in this spirit that teachers are encouraged to use journaling for cumulative review and in support of teaching test-specific thinking. There are multiple opportunities to take advantage of this type of learning, which the following sections describe.

Journaling During Cumulative Review

Journaling fits into every phase of cumulative review. In the first phase (record), students record what they remember about a topic that has been previously introduced to them. As described previously, this step can take different forms, but all forms can be recorded in journals.

During the second phase (review), students examine or test their understanding of the content. As described previously, the teacher might engage students in tasks such as asking inferential questions, generating and defending claims, comparing the current topic with previous topics, and so on. These are all activities that are made more effective if students record their deliberations and conclusions in journals.

The final phase of the cumulative-review process (revise) is designed to help students alter and enhance their knowledge of the topic. This part of the cumulative-review process is highly amenable to journaling. If students systematically record their revisions of thinking on a topic, they will have a detailed, longitudinal record of their understanding of the various topics they encountered in class.

Journaling About Item Frames

There are many ways teachers can use journaling to enhance instruction on item frames, such as the following.

- Students who are struggling with an item can write about the aspects of the item they do not understand. Where do they get stuck? What information or skill would help?
- Students can journal about their emotions associated with test taking. What feelings do they have before, during, and after a test? If they experience anxiety, does anything lessen or increase it? This can help anxious or timid test takers process their feelings and find healthy ways to cope with them.
- Students can use journaling to take a deeper look at the results of a recent test. Which items were they successful with? Which items were a struggle? Students can begin to explore whether the difficulty of missed items was rooted in a misunderstanding of content or a misunderstanding of the item's schema.
- Students can celebrate and reflect on their success with item frames. If they have recently begun to experience success with either a frame type or an aspect of the content, they can write about what has made the difference and how it feels.

Journaling to Reflect on Metacognitive Skills

Journaling lends itself to reinforcing *metacognitive skills*. Such skills are used to examine and improve one's own thinking. Table 6.1 describes ten important metacognitive skills for students.

Like with academic skills, students should receive direct instruction on these skills before they are expected to use them. Teachers and schools can and should create proficiency scales for these skills or use predeveloped scales from an expert source (for example, Peak Curriculum; www.peakcurriculum.com), which enable students to track their effectiveness at using these skills over time.

Once students have a general understanding of these metacognitive skills and strategies for enacting them, teachers can engage them in classroom activities that encourage the use of a particular metacognitive skill. Three of the ten metacognitive

TABLE 6.1: Metacognitive Skills

METACOGNITIVE SKILL	DESCRIPTION
Staying focused when answers and solutions are not immediately apparent	This skill helps students overcome obstacles and stay focused when challenges arise. It also helps students to recognize how much effort they are putting into accomplishing a specific task.
Pushing the limits of one's knowledge and skills	This skill helps students set goals and engage in tasks that are personally challenging. When using this skill, students will strive to learn more and accomplish more.
Generating and pursuing one's own standards for performance	This skill enables students to envision and articulate criteria for what a successful project will look like.
Seeking incremental steps	This skill helps students take on complex tasks using small incremental steps so they do not become overwhelmed by the task as a whole.
Seeking accuracy	This skill helps students vet sources of information for reliability and verify information by consulting multiple sources known to be reliable.
Seeking clarity	This skill helps students identify points of confusion when they are learning new information. This allows students to independently seek a deeper understanding.
Resisting impulsivity	When faced with a desire to form a quick conclusion, this skill helps students refrain from doing so until they can gather more relevant information prior to taking action.
Seeking cohesion and coherence	When students are creating something with a number of interacting parts, this skill helps them monitor the relationships between what they are currently doing and the overall intent of the project in which they are engaged.
Setting goals and making plans	This skill helps students set short- and long-term goals, create timelines or blueprints, monitor progress, and make necessary adjustments.
Growth mindset thinking	This skill helps students take on challenging tasks with an attitude that helps them succeed, even when confronted by major obstacles.

Source: © 2017 by Marzano Resources. Adapted with permission.

skills have particular applications with item frames: (1) staying focused when answers and solutions are not immediately apparent, (2) seeking clarity, and (3) seeking accuracy. All three of these help students when they are working with particularly complex item frames. For example, if students are working on an item that is particularly difficult, the teacher might briefly remind them to stay focused when answers and solutions are not immediately apparent. After students complete the item, the teacher might ask them to reflect on the extent to which they used that metacognitive skill.

Finding Time for Journaling

While there is no single best way or time to use journals, the following list represents common ways teachers employ them.

- **At the beginning and end of the day:** At the beginning of the day, students can journal to bring focus and intention to the day. They can also review entries from the previous day to bring to mind any relevant questions or ideas from the day before. Journaling at the end of the day offers students a chance to review the day's learning and check in regarding their progress on goals. It also offers students an easy way to pick up where they left off.

- **Anytime students engage in cumulative review:** As mentioned previously, students can use journaling to engage in any of the three phases of cumulative review. Both journaling and reviewing old journal entries can help students accomplish review tasks prompted by the teacher, such as making direct or abstract comparisons between a new topic and one that was covered earlier in the school year. Finally, a journal is an excellent place to record and reflect on their revisions of previous learning.

- **Anytime students interact with item frames:** After working with item frames, students can write about their anxieties or fears with testing, areas of confusion regarding content or item schemas, and new insights or understandings that led to success.

- **Anytime an activity occurs where a metacognitive skill might be involved:** Metacognitive skills can be used in a wide variety of activities. For example, a teacher might ask students to employ the skill of resisting impulsivity when playing an academic game by refraining from yelling out the answer to a question the teacher asked another student. When a teacher has cued students to use a particular metacognitive skill with a specific task, students can evaluate their action in their journals.

QUESTIONING TECHNIQUES

Teachers ask many questions during any given class period, many of which they think of and design on the spot (see *Questioning Sequences in the Classroom*; Marzano & Simms, 2014). There is nothing wrong with this practice. However, with a little forethought and planning, teachers can embed the concept of item frames in the types of questions they ask to dramatically increase the level of rigor required while reinforcing the notion that test items require a specific type of thinking. There are a number of ways that a teacher can design such questions, three of which we explore in the following sections.

Students Answer a Question and Then Verify With Evidence

The simplest way to mirror test-specific thinking is to ask students to provide the evidence for their answers to a question or explain the reasoning they used to come up with their answers. Recall from previous discussions that many types of items on large-scale assessments require students to provide evidence for their answers. To illustrate, in an ELA class, assume that students have just finished a story. The teacher asks, "How does the narrator's point of view influence how the events are described?" Students answer the question individually, perhaps in writing. They might also share their answers with one or more of their peers. After they construct and share their answers, the teacher gives another direction: "Identify specific sections of the text that provide support for your answers." Again, students can share their responses with peers.

If a particular question doesn't lend itself to providing evidence for the answer, as depicted in this ELA example, then the teacher can ask students to explain the reasoning behind their answers. To illustrate, consider the following mathematics question: "Joe bought a gallon of milk for $2.79 and some containers of yogurt for $0.39 each. He paid a total of $5.13 for these items. How many containers of yogurt did Joe buy?" Again, each student would answer this question independently and then share their answer in some way. Next, the teacher would tell students to explain the reasoning behind their calculations. Students with the correct answer of 6 might have an explanation like, "If Joe spent $5.13 all together and $2.79 of that was for a gallon of milk, then there was only $2.34 with which to buy containers of yogurt. If each container cost $0.39, then Joe must have bought 6 of them because $2.34 divided by $0.39 equals 6."

Prompting students to systematically explain and defend the reasoning behind their answers forces them to revisit and perhaps revise conclusions they have drawn.

Students Agree or Disagree With the Teacher's Answer

A level up in terms of the complexity of thinking required of students is for the teacher to provide an answer to a particular question and have the students agree or disagree with it and then provide evidence for their position. To illustrate, assume students read a short passage and then the teacher asks, "What is the meaning of the word *deliberate* as it is used in the fourth paragraph on page 12 of the story?" This question uses the *meaning* item frame, where students are charged with discerning the meaning of a particular word in a passage. Rather than simply having students immediately answer the question, the teacher says they think the intended meaning of *deliberate* is that it is synonymous with *important*. The teacher adds, "If you agree with me, identify the evidence from specific parts of the story that supports this answer. If you don't agree with me, describe what you think the intended meaning is and cite the specific parts of the text that support your answer."

When this questioning approach is used, it forces students to consider multiple possible answers, which, by definition, makes the task more complex in that it requires not only the generation of an answer but also the comparison of answers.

Students Select From Multiple Possible Answers and Provide Evidence

The type of questioning technique that most clearly mirrors test-specific thinking is for the teacher to present a question along with multiple options for the correct answer. Students select the correct answer and provide evidence for their answers.

To illustrate, assume that an ELA teacher is having students read *Charlie and the Chocolate Factory* (Dahl, 1964) and wants them to recognize that author Roald Dahl had reasons for the events he portrayed in the story. The general topic the teacher wishes to emphasize is that writers use the events in their stories to communicate specific ideas. To demonstrate this, the teacher might ask students to explain why Charlie won the contest. Of course, a very straightforward and maybe even typical approach is to simply ask students, "Why do you think Charlie won the contest?" To answer this question, a student must recall what happened in the story and then translate those events into a logical reason why Charlie won the contest. Again, this is a legitimate practice in terms of asking questions in the classroom. To make the question more rigorous in terms of students' thinking, though, the teacher could construct two or more possible answers and present them along with the question, like the following.

> *We know that Charlie won the contest. Which of the following reasons do you think is the best answer to why Charlie won the contest?*
>
> a. *Charlie behaved well, but the other children did not.*
>
> b. *Willy Wonka saw something in Charlie that made him admire Charlie.*
>
> c. *Because of Charlie's background, he appreciated the small things in life.*

Students now must consider three possible reasons. As before, they still must recall the events that occurred in the story and think of them in terms of reasons why Charlie won the contest, but they must also determine which of these statements is best supported by the events as a reason for Charlie winning the contest.

By presenting multiple possible answers and requiring students to determine which is best, the teacher dramatically raises the complexity of thinking required of students and, of course, mirrors the types of tasks students will encounter in large-scale assessments. The more alternative answers the teacher presents to students, the more complex the thinking required is. For example, the following question requires even more complex thinking than the previous example.

We know that Charlie won the contest. Which of the following reasons do you think is the best answer to why Charlie won the contest?

   a. *Charlie behaved well, but the other children did not.*

   b. *Willy Wonka saw something in Charlie that made him admire Charlie.*

   c. *Because of Charlie's background, he appreciated the small things in life.*

   d. *Unlike the other children who tried to cheat, Charlie remained true to his principles.*

   e. *Charlie's family was extremely poor, and he put his family's needs before his own desires.*

Here, students must analyze the events in the story relative to five different ways of describing why Charlie won the contest.

GUIDED DISCOURSE

While the cumulative-review process, if done systematically (such as once per week), provides students with in-depth opportunities to examine and refine their current understanding of academic content, there are also many other opportunities where a teacher can use a streamlined version of this process. These opportunities occur during daily interactions with students. Specifically, anytime teachers ask students to read, watch, or listen to new information or engage in some type of task, it is an opportunity for teachers and students to implement an abbreviated form of cumulative review referred to as *guided discourse*. The following sections introduce and explain the steps of guided discourse through the lens of a mathematics example and then consider an ELA example.

Guided Discourse With Mathematics Items

Like questioning techniques, this interaction requires a conscious effort on the part of the teacher, since, most of the time, these opportunities receive little attention and are addressed in a fairly superficial manner. To illustrate the typical approach to classroom discourse, assume a teacher has asked students to solve a few mathematics problems involving equivalent fractions. The teacher might then ask students to share their answers with the entire class or a small group of peers, or both. While this is a useful activity, consider the students' thinking throughout the process: Each student generates an answer to each problem and has an opportunity to hear other students' answers, but the thinking stops there. Students simply answer the questions and hear other answers. Again, this is a useful activity, but it does little to help students move beyond their initial thinking. Guided discourse moves thinking and learning to deeper levels.

When employing guided discourse, the teacher begins by presenting the mathematics problems in the same way as in the first scenario. For example, assume the teacher asked students to solve the following three problems, all of which deal with equivalent fractions.

1. Lily has $3/8$ of a box of pencils. She wants to share them equally among her 4 friends. What fraction of the box does each friend get?
2. Sarah is baking a cake, and the recipe calls for $3/4$ cup of flour. She only has a $1/2$ cup measuring cup. How many times does she need to use the $1/2$ cup measuring cup to get the right amount of flour?
3. Mia wants to divide a roll of ribbon into equal pieces for her art project. If she cuts the ribbon into 5 equal pieces and uses 3 of them, what fraction of the ribbon did she use?

After students have completed these problems, the teacher asks them to state their answers and possibly share them with peers. Again, this is what occurred in the first scenario. However, in the guided discourse scenario, the teacher follows up by asking students to describe the thinking they used to produce their answers and then interacts with them while they are providing their explanations. To illustrate, consider the first problem about Lily sharing her pencils with her friends. After students have shared their answers with peers, the teacher directs a discussion like the following.

Teacher: Tell me what you did to solve this problem.

Student A: Well, I multiplied the $3/8$ by 4.

Teacher: What did you get?

Student A: $3/8$ times $4/1$ = $12/8$ or 1 and $4/8$, but this answer doesn't make any sense to me.

Teacher: Why did you choose to do it that way?

Student A: Those were the numbers in the problem. I just figured that we were supposed to multiply them to come up with an answer.

Teacher: OK, I see the thinking you were using, but it looks like it didn't get to an answer that makes sense for you. Focusing on only the numbers in a problem while performing a random mathematical operation doesn't seem to work well. Did anyone else take another approach?

Student B: I tried to figure out what I was supposed to do before I performed any mathematical operations. I thought that the problem gave us a little bit of information about how many pencils there were, but you had to figure out the rest.

Teacher: So where did you start?

Student B: I knew that Lily only has ⅜ of the pencils in the box. I think that's an important part of the problem. So we don't know how many total pencils there are. But that's OK since the problem is about how you break up the ⅜ into 4 equal parts. At first, I thought I had to figure out the number of pencils each friend gets, but actually, the problem only talks about what fraction of the total box each friend gets. Then I knew that to get the answer, all I had to do was divide the ⅜ into 4 parts.

Teacher: So how do you do that?

Student B: That's easy. You first write the problem as ⅜ divided by 4 or ⁽³⁄₈⁾/4. But when you are dividing a fraction by a whole number, you have to multiply the fraction by the reciprocal of the whole number. So ⅜ times ¼.

Teacher: What do you get?

Student B: 3/32.

Teacher: So explain the answer in words to us.

Student B: The answer is each of the four friends would get 3/32 of the pencils in the box.

Teacher: Good. But let's take it a step further. How many pencils does each student get if there are 64 pencils in the box?

Student B: You would multiply 3/32 by 64/1. You multiply the numerators first. That's 3 times 64, which is 192. You then divide this by 32, which gives us 6. So each of the 4 friends gets 6 pencils. All together, the 4 friends share 24 pencils, and 24 pencils is ⅜ of the 64 total pencils.

Teacher: OK, let's summarize some things we've learned. Let's start with things that don't work well. It looks like it's not a good idea to focus only on the numbers in the problem. But a strategy that looks like it works pretty well is to read the whole problem and try to get a sense of the big picture. One part of that big picture was to see that you were working with a fraction of the whole. In this case, the fraction was ⅜ of the whole. The next part of the problem was to divide that fraction of the whole into 4 equal parts. After that, the problem amounted to remembering some of the rules about fractions. One rule is when *you divide a fraction by a whole number, you take the reciprocal of the whole number and multiply it by the fraction.*

Now, take a few moments to share what you've learned about problems like this by answering three questions: (1) How was my thinking right about these types of problems? (2) How was my thinking wrong about these types of problems? (3) What new things have I learned about these types of problems?

Notice that the teacher did four things during guided discourse: (1) probed students' thinking; (2) restated or rephrased students' thinking to emphasize errors and misconceptions; (3) restated or rephrased students' thinking to emphasize useful facts, strategies, and insights; and (4) asked students to state what they were right about in their thinking, what they were wrong about in their thinking, and what new ideas they have about the topic.

We'll go into more detail about each of these four parts separately.

Probe Students' Thinking

Probing students' thinking is the part of the process that requires the most artistry on the part of the teacher. Fundamentally, the teacher is trying to use their interactions with students to tease out important things students should know about the content being addressed as well as common errors and misconceptions students have run into about the content being addressed. To this end, it is useful for teachers to think through important aspects of the content and common errors and misconceptions about the topic.

In the example we have been discussing, the content being addressed is equivalent fractions. Prior to presenting the problems to students, the teacher might simply think through what to emphasize and what errors and omissions to make students aware of. It can be helpful for teachers to use an artificial intelligence (AI) chatbot as a thought partner by querying it on these two issues. Following are the results of an AI query for things to emphasize about equivalent fractions (OpenAI, 2023).

 What should teachers highlight when teaching fourth-grade students about equivalent fractions?

- Begin by explaining that equivalent fractions are fractions that represent the same amount or value, even though they may look different.
- Teach students that finding equivalent fractions involves multiplying or dividing both the numerator and denominator by the same nonzero number.
- Emphasize the importance of finding common multiples of the numerator and denominator to create equivalent fractions.

Supporting and Integrating the Use of Item Frames

- Show how to create equivalent fractions by multiplying both the numerator and denominator by the same number.
- Use visual models, such as fraction bars or circles, to illustrate this concept.
- Explain that equivalent fractions can also be created by reducing fractions to their simplest form (lowest terms).
- Reinforce the concept that the greatest common factor (GCF) is used to simplify fractions.

Next, consider the results of an AI query about common misconceptions and errors regarding equivalent fractions (OpenAI, 2023).

What are some common errors and misconceptions fourth graders have when learning about equivalent fractions?

Believing That Larger Numerators Mean Larger Fractions: Some students may think that a fraction with a larger numerator (for example, 5/7) is always larger than a fraction with a smaller numerator (for example, 3/7). They may not realize that the denominator also plays a crucial role in determining the fraction's size.

- **Address:** Emphasize that fractions with the same denominator can be compared based on their numerators. A larger numerator means a larger fraction, but only when the denominators are the same.

Ignoring the Denominator: Some students may focus solely on the numerator when trying to find equivalent fractions and may change the numerator without considering the denominator.

- **Address:** Reinforce the idea that both the numerator and denominator must be scaled by the same factor to maintain equivalence.

Confusing Equivalent Fractions With Simplified Fractions: Students might think that equivalent fractions and simplified fractions are the same thing. They may believe that if two fractions don't look the same, they can't be equivalent.

- **Address:** Clarify the difference between equivalent fractions (which represent the same value) and simplified fractions (which are in their simplest form but might not look the same).

Limited Understanding of Multiplication and Division: Students may struggle to grasp the concept of multiplying or dividing both the numerator and denominator to find equivalent fractions. They might not see the connection between multiplication and division in this context.

- **Address:** Use concrete examples, visual models, and hands-on activities to illustrate the process of multiplying or dividing to find equivalent fractions.

Inconsistent Use of Equivalent Fractions: Students may use equivalent fractions in one context but not in another. For example, they may correctly find equivalent fractions for addition but forget to do so when comparing fractions.
- **Address:** Encourage students to consistently apply the concept of equivalent fractions across various mathematical operations and problem-solving situations.

Misunderstanding Mixed Numbers: Students may struggle to convert mixed numbers to improper fractions and vice versa. They may incorrectly assume that mixed numbers cannot have equivalent forms.
- **Address:** Teach students the relationship between mixed numbers and improper fractions and how both can have equivalent forms.

Overgeneralizing Equivalent Fractions: Some students may try to make any fraction equivalent to any other fraction by randomly multiplying or dividing the numerator and denominator.
- **Address:** Teach students that equivalent fractions must maintain the same ratio between the numerator and denominator. Not all fractions can be made equivalent to one another.

Lack of Visualizing Equivalent Fractions: Some students may find it challenging to visualize equivalent fractions using fraction models or number lines.
- **Address:** Continue to use visual aids and hands-on activities to help students develop a concrete understanding of equivalent fractions.

Notice that for each error or misconception listed, the chatbot provided ways for the teacher to help alleviate the problem. Knowing this information generated from AI can help teachers look for things to emphasize when interacting with students during guided discourse. While AI has been fairly reliable when responding to our queries about K–12 academic content, teachers should still carefully examine the output to check for errors and inaccuracies.

Restate or Rephrase Students' Thinking to Emphasize Errors and Misconceptions

Emphasizing errors and misconceptions is a critical part of the instructional process because it is common for students at a given age to have similar misconceptions and make similar errors. When considering errors and misconceptions, it's important to recognize the differences between errors in information (formally referred to as *declarative knowledge*) and errors in skills and processes (formally referred to as *procedural knowledge*). Declarative knowledge involves things like the concepts of a plot, setting, character, and theme. Students can have misconceptions about these concepts. For example, relative to the concept of setting, some students might have misconceptions that setting is simply the details behind the story, as opposed to knowing the setting contributes to the mood or supports the narrative.

Procedural knowledge includes skills and processes such as summarizing information in a passage or executing two-column addition. Errors in procedural knowledge are sometimes very hard to detect and correct. Some types of errors in procedural knowledge are referred to as *buggy algorithms*. The term *bugs* is actually a technical one relative to procedural knowledge and was made popular by the National Research Council at the turn of the 21st century. The National Research Council (2004) explained that bugs occur when students attempt to apply a conventional algorithm without conceptually grasping why and how the algorithm works. For example, teachers have long wrestled with the frequent difficulties that second and third graders have with multidigit subtraction in problems such as the following.

$$\begin{array}{r} 51 \\ -\ 14 \\ \hline \end{array}$$

A common error students make is:

$$\begin{array}{r} 51 \\ -\ 14 \\ \hline 43 \end{array}$$

Here, the student has erroneously subtracted 1 from 4 in the ones column when they should have subtracted 4 from 11 by borrowing from the tens. Bugs are often resilient and persistent. Consider how reasonable the preceding procedure is. The algorithm some students use might be stated as, "When given numbers to subtract, you always subtract the smaller number from the larger number."

The important point here is that students become aware of common errors and misconceptions that people make in general and that they make in particular. Being aware of errors and misconceptions is a critical part of learning because it helps you know what *not* to do, which, in turn, sharpens your understanding of what *to* do.

Restate or Rephrase Students' Thinking to Emphasize Important Facts, Strategies, and Insights

Calling students' attention to important facts, strategies, and insights is the counterbalance to identifying errors and misconceptions, since it emphasizes what *to* do as opposed to what *not* to do. In the equivalent fractions example, the teacher emphasized the fact that a good strategy is to read the entire problem first to get a sense of the information you are given and what you are expected to do with it. The teacher also emphasized some important facts about dividing a fraction by a whole number.

A beneficial practice when rephrasing or restating useful things gleaned from guided discourse with students is to record these insights. The teacher might do this immediately after interacting with students on a particular issue. This might be as simple as writing these insights on a whiteboard. Going a step further, the teacher can permanently archive these insights by recording them on a Google document that all students have access to at any time.

Ask Students to Describe What They Were Right About, What They Were Wrong About, and What New Ideas They Have

This last part of guided discourse is a direct corollary to the revise phase of cumulative review. To cue students, the teacher might simply pose the following questions to students at the end of a guided discourse session.

Based on our discussion:
- *What were you right about?*
- *What were you wrong about?*
- *What new ideas do you have about this topic?*

When used during guided discourse, students can simply verbalize their answers to these questions in small groups. However, on occasion, the teacher might ask students to take out their journals and record their answers to these questions.

Guided Discourse With ELA Items

When dealing with ELA items, guided discourse follows the same steps: (1) probe students' thinking; (2) restate or rephrase students' thinking to emphasize errors and misconceptions; (3) restate or rephrase students' thinking to emphasize useful facts, strategies, and insights; and (4) ask students to articulate what they were right about in their thinking, what they were wrong about in their thinking, and what new ideas they have about the topic.

To illustrate how guided discourse manifests in ELA, consider the following scenario. Assume that a middle school ELA teacher has students read an expository passage. Before the students begin reading, the teacher informs them they should be reading with an eye toward determining the author's purpose. She has provided each student with a copy of the passage on which they can make notes. She tells them to look for textual cues regarding the author's purpose. When they find those clues, they should make annotations in their copy of the passage.

In preparation for using guided discourse during this assignment, the teacher makes two simple queries to an AI chatbot. The first query deals with those things that should be emphasized when teaching middle school students about the author's purpose; the AI-generated response follows (OpenAI, 2023).

 What should a teacher emphasize when helping students learn how to identify an author's purpose?

Definition of Author's Purpose: Start by explaining that an author's purpose refers to the reason why they wrote a particular text. Authors typically write for one or more of the following main purposes:

- **To Inform:** The author wants to provide information, facts, or explanations about a topic.
- **To Persuade:** The author aims to convince the reader of a particular point of view or to take a specific action.
- **To Entertain:** The author's primary goal is to engage and amuse the reader.
- **To Describe:** The author intends to paint a vivid picture or create a sensory experience for the reader.
- **To Explain:** The author's purpose is to clarify a concept or process.
- **To Narrate:** The author tells a story or recounts events.

Textual Clues and Evidence: Teach students to look for textual clues or evidence within the text that can help them determine the author's purpose. These clues may include:

- **Key Phrases:** Words or phrases that indicate the author's intent (for example, "In conclusion," "I believe that," "For example").
- **Tone and Mood:** The emotional tone of the text can provide insights into the author's purpose (for example, a persuasive tone for persuasion).
- **Genre:** The genre of the text (for example, a news article, opinion piece, or story) can suggest the author's purpose.
- **Examples and Illustrations:** The type and frequency of examples or illustrations used can hint at the purpose (for example, informative texts may use data or statistics).

Consider the Audience: Emphasize that an author's purpose can be influenced by the intended audience. Authors may adapt their purpose based on whether they are writing for children, adults, experts, or a general audience.

The second query deals with common errors and misconceptions students have when looking for the author's purpose (OpenAI, 2023).

What are some common errors and misconceptions fourth-grade students commonly have about author purpose?

Confusing Plot With Purpose: Some students may think that the plot of the story (what happens in the story) is the same as the author's purpose. They might not differentiate between the events in the story and why the author wrote the story.

- **Address:** Clarify the distinction between the plot (the story's events) and the author's purpose (the reason the author wrote the story).

Assuming Every Text Has a Single Purpose: Students may mistakenly believe that every text has only one purpose. They might not recognize that an author can have multiple purposes within a single text.

- **Address:** Explain that authors often have more than one purpose, such as to inform and entertain simultaneously, and show examples in various texts.

Misinterpreting Persuasive Elements as Informative: Some students may have difficulty distinguishing between informative and persuasive texts. They might think that any text that provides information is purely informative, even if it also tries to persuade the reader.

- **Address:** Teach students to look for persuasive language and arguments that indicate an author's intent to convince the reader.

Equating Author's Opinion With Purpose: Students may assume that the author's opinion or beliefs are the sole purpose of a text. They might not recognize that authors can write about topics they don't personally endorse.

- **Address:** Help students understand that an author's purpose can go beyond expressing their personal beliefs and may involve informing, entertaining, or narrating.

Overgeneralizing Author's Purpose: Some students may generalize the author's purpose based on a single piece of evidence or passage from the text. They might overlook the broader intention behind the entire work.

- **Address:** Encourage students to consider the text as a whole and look for recurring themes, tone, and patterns of argumentation to determine the overall purpose.

Ignoring the Influence of Audience: Students might overlook the role of the intended audience in shaping the author's purpose. They may assume that a text serves the same purpose for all readers.

- **Address:** Highlight how the author's purpose can be influenced by the intended audience and guide students in considering the audience's needs and expectations.

Relying Solely on Personal Feelings: Some students may determine the author's purpose based on their own emotional response to the text rather than analyzing the text objectively.

- **Address:** Teach students to use textual evidence, tone, and structure as the basis for identifying the author's purpose, rather than relying solely on personal feelings.

Not Considering Context: Students may overlook the historical, cultural, or societal context in which a text was written, leading to misinterpretations of the author's purpose.

- **Address:** Encourage students to research and discuss the context of a text to gain a deeper understanding of the author's motivations.

The teacher studies this AI-generated information to be well prepared for the interactions with students.

After students have read the passage, annotated their texts regarding evidence, and generated their conclusions about the author's purpose, the teacher asks them to share their answers in small groups. After these interactions, the teacher starts the guided discourse process by asking questions and then probing students' thinking regarding their answers.

The teacher starts by asking if anyone had trouble figuring out the author's purpose. A couple of students raise their hands, and the teacher invites them to share. One student says that it seems like there were different purposes in different parts of the text. Other students chime in with similar responses, saying that it seemed like the author was trying to provide a great deal of information in some parts of the text, while in other parts, it seemed like the author was trying to persuade the reader. The teacher uses this discussion to reinforce the fact that authors can have more than one purpose. Often, an author might have a main purpose, but then different parts of the text might represent different purposes. The teacher uses this discussion to point out sections of the text that represent different purposes. Additionally, the teacher writes the following on the whiteboard: "Authors commonly have more than one purpose for their writing."

One student is adamant about the fact that the author's main purpose must be to show that global warming is currently the biggest threat to Earth's well-being. The student even points to a section of the text where the author states that this is their opinion. The teacher discusses this with the student and agrees that, yes, this seems to be the author's opinion, but follows up by asking if the author's opinion is the same as the author's purpose. The class joins the discussion, and as a group, they come to the joint conclusion that the author's opinion probably influences the author's purpose, but they aren't the same. In this case, one of the author's purposes was to provide new information to readers that would influence their thinking. The teacher writes on the whiteboard: "The author's opinion is not necessarily the same as the author's purpose."

After the teacher has emphasized a few other things, they ask students to reflect on the following three questions.

1. What were you right about in your thinking?
2. What were you wrong about in your thinking?
3. What new ideas do you have about this topic?

The teacher has students return to their small groups, where they share their answers to these questions and then record what they have learned in their journals.

THE SUCCESSIVE RELEARNING INSTRUCTIONAL CYCLE

In the introductory comments about cumulative review, we noted that it falls into a general category that cognitive scientists refer to as *successive relearning*. With the addition of the other activities and strategies discussed in this chapter, it is now possible to articulate a cycle of instructional activities that we call the *successive relearning instructional cycle*. This cycle applies to every subject at every grade level. We believe that it is a system every teacher can and should use throughout the school year on a systematic basis. There are four components to this cycle: (1) identification of topics, (2) weekly cumulative review, (3) continuous journaling, and (4) planned and spontaneous use of questioning techniques and guided discourse.

Identification of Topics

The successive relearning instructional cycle begins with an articulation of the key topics that teachers will address throughout the school year. We provided an example of such an articulation of nineteen fifth-grade mathematics topics in the section Frequency of Cumulative Review (page 69). This is foundational; the list of measurement topics defines the topics students must master in that course, and thus, those topics should be the subject of the successive relearning instructional cycle. Every teacher should begin each school year knowing the specific topics they will address in the successive relearning instructional cycle. Ideally, each topic will be accompanied by a proficiency scale with an item frame embedded at score 3.0 of the scale.

Weekly Cumulative Review

Cumulative review should occur on a weekly basis, as described previously (page 69). During weekly cumulative-review sessions, the teacher uses the three phases of cumulative review to address new review topics and make connections to previously reviewed topics. By the end of the school year, all identified topics should have been the focus of cumulative review, and connections should have been made with other topics.

Continuous Journaling

Journaling should occur continuously throughout the school year—certainly during the phases of cumulative review. Additionally, it should occur between weekly cumulative-review sessions as opportunities and needs arise (see page 74). Ideally, students should journal once daily.

Planned and Spontaneous Use of Questioning Techniques and Guided Discourse

Between cumulative-review sessions, teachers should plan to use questioning techniques (page 74) and guided discourse (page 77), as described in this chapter. As the name implies, *planned questions* are those a teacher identifies when planning for an upcoming lesson. Here, teachers articulate specific questions at specific times in a lesson. Additionally, teachers should take advantage of serendipitous opportunities to use questioning techniques and guided discourse. For example, an interaction with the class about a specific topic might lead the teacher to ask a specific type of question at that particular moment. In effect, questioning and guided discourse are the tools teachers use to keep academic content continually in the forefront of students' thinking.

ADAPTATIONS FROM THE FIELD

In the previous chapters, we presented different ways teachers might use item frames, and in this chapter, we present instructional strategies that support and augment their use. While we discussed all these elements as separate topics, in the classroom, teachers frequently combine them in unique ways that pertain to the needs of their particular students. They also present them to their students in unique ways. Here, we present some examples of how classroom teachers use the various elements discussed in this book and the way they present them to their students. Each example is derived from teachers' firsthand observations in their classrooms.

Brandon Peterson

Brandon Peterson is a fifth-grade teacher at Woodland Elementary School in Aurora, Colorado.

As I step into my fifth-grade classroom, I see a place that is both exciting and engaging, encouraging all my students to explore their curiosities and make meaningful connections to everything they learn. Many aspects of my classroom blend traditional methods with modern, personalized approaches to teaching and learning.

It's a space that comforts students and fosters a desire for learning that is fun, infectious, personal, and passionate.

One noticeable feature is the daily use of test item frames integrated into nearly every lesson. They appear as introductory challenges to review previously learned material or to stimulate thinking before delving into new content, as mid-lesson challenges to prompt students to reflect on and analyze prior learning, or as exit tickets to assess comprehension and identify areas needing further study. The item frames themselves consist of a variety of open-ended, short-answer, or multiple-choice questions, often mirroring the higher-rigor questioning typical of standardized tests or beyond. Frequently, these frames include part A for completing a standard question, part B for deeper analysis of their answer, and sometimes part C for creating their own complementary item frame.

My fifth-grade team and I decided to write many of these frames with real-life connections in mind. For instance, in mathematics, there are a plethora of questions concerning decimals, fractions, and the order of operations, challenging students to apply the mathematics standards they learned throughout the school year to practical, real-world scenarios. One such example involved calculating the volume of folded winter clothes and determining the appropriate box size for storing them over the summer. This exercise not only presented challenges due to the absence of multiple-choice answers but also required students to apply previously learned information in a deeper and realistic context. At the conclusion of the activity, students responded enthusiastically, engaging in a reflective discussion connected to numerous mathematics academic standards in practice. This demonstrates the purpose and positive outcomes of item frames: They spark interest and motivation to learn and apply academic content in meaningful ways. Additionally, they enable us to easily assess students' learning progress, identify gaps, address confusion, and plan next steps effectively.

Initially, test item frames were met with reluctance in our classroom. However, with finesse, consistency, and quality implementation, their value became evident to our fifth-grade team at Woodland Elementary. First, they enhanced transparency in learning; students gained a clearer understanding of content alignment with academic standards, anticipating the lesson's trajectory related to the item frame. Moreover, they fostered a culture where students approached content with increased determination and depth of thought. Students enjoyed tackling item frames, sometimes creating their own, and approached problem solving in innovative ways. This shift was evident in their improved use of discipline-specific language, such as discussing text features and the author's tone with fluency. Students no longer simply answered questions out of habit; they were held to higher rigor, necessitating deeper thinking about the material they were learning.

Additionally, item frames facilitated continual cumulative review, providing students with opportunities for analysis, synthesis, and reflection. This approach significantly enhanced memory retention and prepared students comprehensively for various school and state assessments. Furthermore, consistent practice through daily efforts naturally cultivated advanced problem-solving skills and fostered an internal drive for critical and deep-level thinking—an achievement long sought after in educational settings. Engaging in such higher-level thinking not only made students more academically proficient but also significantly increased their likelihood of growth and success.

In summary, the integration of test item frames has proven transformative in fostering a dynamic learning environment where curiosity thrives and learning is rigorous and meaningful. By infusing real-life contexts into everyday lessons, teachers enable students to engage deeply with academic content and develop the critical-thinking skills essential for lifelong learning. The journey from initial reluctance to enthusiastic adoption underscores the profound impact of these frames, which enhance transparency in learning and empower students to approach challenges with confidence. As educators, we witness firsthand the joy and motivation sparked by these strategies, paving the way for students to become not just test takers but thoughtful problem solvers prepared for academic success and beyond.

Maša Fritz
Maša Fritz is a mathematics teacher working at the Colorado STEM Academy in Westminster, Colorado. Maša works with fifth-, sixth-, and seventh-grade students.

The way I approach cumulative review is mainly through the use of item frames, incorporating them into my cumulative-review process. I'll show you what I've developed over the years. It took some time to set up initially, but now it's much easier. I started by taking the item frames that Bob Marzano posted on our Westminster Public Schools website. I also explored the New Meridian website, which has all the released items from our state end-of-year test, CMAS [Colorado Measures of Academic Success], going back to 2015. I went through every test, categorized every problem, and matched them to our learning targets.

For example, I went through the sixth-grade tests and compiled all the relevant data into one slideshow. These slides featured released CMAS problems, beginning in 2015, organized by the learning targets. My next target for sixth grade was dividing fractions, so I gathered all the item frames related to that concept and placed them in one slideshow. I housed everything in a single resource. Some slides included multiple skills, like volume and fractions or expressions, which are all sixth-grade targets. I created similar compilations for grades 5 and 7.

Some problems came directly from Bob Marzano's item frames, and they were very similar to what students would encounter on the test. We practiced skills like multiple-select questions, where students may have more than one correct answer, as well as problems where they type in explanations and use mathematics symbols. That's how it all began—I developed slideshows for each target and included all relevant item frames. Now, when I do cumulative reviews, which I conduct every Monday, I select specific frames for the students to work on each week. As we progress through the school year, I have more targets and problems to choose from, pulling in problems from September, December, and so on, ensuring consistent review.

Now, to focus on the three stages of cumulative learning—record, review, and revise—I'll walk you through what this looks like from the perspective of a student. Since September, I've been using a folder to organize all the item frames we worked on each week. For instance, I print a problem, and we begin by recording: reading the problem together, identifying the skills required, and recalling relevant targets we learned previously. If students see a percentage in the problem, we discuss how it relates to percentages and might draw a ratio table, for example, to review.

The review process comes next, where we delve deeper into the problem. This part isn't just about solving the problem but teaching students to deconstruct the frame itself—understanding what type of problem it is before diving into the content. For instance, if a problem involves percentages, we review how to solve percentage problems before attempting the solution.

Finally, the revise phase is where we go over any mistakes and fix them together. We discuss misconceptions, adjust our work, and reflect on what changed from the beginning of the lesson to the end. Sometimes, I'll give them a mix of problems with multiple skills, and we discuss the structure—whether it's multiple choice, multiple select, or open response.

Over time, students become quicker at solving these problems because they recognize the structure and know what's being asked. This practice builds confidence and helps reduce test anxiety. I find that by the time students reach the test, they are much more prepared because they've been practicing these problems since September. They're familiar with the format and the content, which allows them to approach the test with less stress.

If I were to give advice to new teachers or those unfamiliar with cumulative review or item frames, I would suggest starting small. Focus on one item frame and slowly build from there. Ask for help from colleagues and collaborate with other teachers. Everyone approaches this a bit differently, so sharing ideas can be incredibly helpful. Additionally, spend time understanding the structure of the test before worrying too much about content. Once you're familiar with how problems are set up, you can then incorporate content more effectively.

Ultimately, this method helps prepare students for both the content and the structure of the test. It's about building both the skills and the confidence they need to succeed.

Elizabeth Gallegos

Elizabeth Gallegos teaches seventh-, eighth-, and ninth-grade literacy at the Colorado STEM Academy in Westminster, Colorado.

To me, the record phase of cumulative review is the first step when introducing something new. Recording sets the foundation. But it doesn't stop there—it spirals, especially in literacy. We're constantly reviewing and recording in different ways because everything connects.

For example, my first ELA unit is usually on research. Even though we're not explicitly teaching research later in the school year, students still practice the language and concepts while working on other units. This continuous cycle of learning keeps our targets active all year long. I always aim to talk, record, and integrate what we've already learned, making sure it's all connected and not isolated. So, the record and review phases of cumulative review always went together for me.

As for the revise phase of cumulative review, revising isn't just about fixing errors; it's about deepening understanding. In literacy, for example, students may grasp a theme in a small passage, but as the school year progresses, we revise that thinking to see how the theme connects to the entire novel or how conflict relates to theme. It's about making connections and building depth.

I've found that this process—constantly revisiting and revising ideas—helps students see that concepts are not isolated but rather part of a larger, interconnected understanding. It's been a game changer for me in terms of planning. Revising doesn't just mean saying, "This is wrong, let's fix it"—it's more about engaging deeply and evolving our thinking.

My students have data notebooks, and we use these alongside proficiency scales. I'm intentional about making sure we revisit past work, like having them highlight notes or refer back to their notebooks. For example, if we're discussing conflict, I might have them underline earlier notes and make connections to the current unit. Cumulative review is embedded throughout the school year, not as a separate task but as an integral part of learning.

Cumulative review plays a key role in connecting past knowledge with new material. For instance, when we study theme in fiction, I ask them how that understanding applies to nonfiction. It's about revising and applying prior knowledge in different contexts, which is crucial for deep learning.

Regarding item frames, they help ensure that I'm intentional with how I ask students to demonstrate their knowledge. They've provided consistency and focus, especially when I felt a bit scattered as a first-year teacher. I use item frames in tests, assignments, and daily questions. They're all about giving students a structured way to show what they've learned, and they align well with district resources and high-stakes testing like CMAS.

Chris Tidd
Chris Tidd is a teacher in Westminster, Colorado.

The process of reviewing and revisiting content is ongoing. It's essential to remember that sometimes, what seems tricky at first might make more sense after some time has passed. That's why cumulative review is important—learning happens over time, not just in isolated moments.

As for how I structure record, review, and revise throughout the week, it varies. Mondays are a great time to introduce new content—usually vocabulary or lighter material to ease into the week. I think routines are key so that students know Monday is when we'll learn new words and put them into practice. Technology, especially AI tools like ChatGPT, has made this even easier by helping me create customized reading passages with the vocabulary we're learning right from day one.

In my teaching, I use project-based learning. By definition, projects are more organic, and entry points can vary depending on the project. But in any case, having a structured routine is crucial. At the beginning of the school year, when trust, relationships, or routines haven't yet been established, teaching a new concept can feel impossible. Once those structures are in place, students have somewhere to store and organize their learning, which makes the process more effective.

A safe, inclusive, and trusting classroom environment is equally important. Students, especially those with difficult home lives, need a space where they can focus on learning without distractions. My classroom is designed to be that kind of sanctuary for them.

We also use data binders regularly. Students track their progress with tools like Empower, our learning management system, and can see which targets they've met and which are ahead. This level of transparency empowers them to take charge of their own education, which is something I find unique to and rewarding in our district.

I incorporate data notebooks and binders daily, at least once or twice a day, particularly on Mondays, when we dive into Empower. Students track things like reading fluency and graph their daily progress. These students, though only nine or ten years old, already have a good sense of what data look like and how to use them to set realistic goals.

In terms of reviewing, I always stress that if you've taken the time to write notes, you should also take time to review them. Revisiting key concepts the next day, or even later in the week, is crucial for memory retention. So, the review process is integrated throughout the day, whether it's reviewing notes or circling back to previous lessons.

Item frames, whether for CMAS or other diagnostic purposes, offer a structured way to check both surface-level understanding and deeper comprehension. For example, evaluating an expression in mathematics requires students to know what *evaluate* means, but it also pushes them to think critically about larger concepts. When students see problems presented in different ways, the goal is to ensure they're not thrown off by unfamiliar formats but can still apply the knowledge they've gained.

I've had instances where students were confused by a different representation of something they understood mathematically. This showed me that while they had learned it, it wasn't fully solidified at their core. So, part of my job is helping them deconstruct the item frame and figure out what's being asked.

For new teachers getting started with item frames and cumulative learning, don't wait until testing season to begin using these tools. Start by understanding what students need to be able to do by the end of a unit, and use formative assessments to track progress. It's all about knowing what your students need, checking in on their learning along the way, and adjusting as needed. While not every student will grasp everything immediately, the goal is to ensure every student makes meaningful growth throughout the school year.

Abigail Anderson

Abigail Anderson is a primary-grade teacher at the Colorado STEM Academy in Westminster, Colorado.

I believe it's essential to integrate cumulative review every day, especially with our youngest learners because they're building foundational skills. We have a dedicated part of each day for cumulative review, which often takes place during morning work. For example, in January, my level 1 students were learning *greater than*, *less than*, and *equal to*. Even though we've moved on from that, we still revisit the concept weekly through activities, such as our "alligator mouths" exercise. This ensures they're continually reviewing and retaining the information.

Typically, we focus intensively on a topic for two to three weeks—depending on how quickly students grasp it—and then we assess them at the end of the unit. Based on the results, I determine which students need more practice and which ones just need quick, periodic reviews to keep the material fresh in their minds. This process really helps them as they prepare for the STAR assessment and the DIBELS assessments, ensuring they remember key concepts like *greater than* months later because we've consistently revisited them.

The record stage of cumulative review happens daily as my students work through new content. The next day, we revisit what we learned and go over any common mistakes. This is the review phase. If a revision is needed after an assessment, we address that as well. If students have mastered the material, we move on but still review it in subsequent weeks to ensure retention. Generally, we aim to introduce two new skills each week, practice them daily, and then build them into future lessons.

Item frames are most commonly used in end-of-unit assessments as well as in mathematics word problems. One major focus for level 1 students is learning how to interpret word problems, which goes beyond just solving equations. They need to understand what the question is asking. For example, they may know that $5 + 15 = 20$, but they need to understand what the question is asking before jumping to the answer. Our item frames help break down these questions, guiding students through each step so they can solve problems methodically.

For example, when faced with an item that says to select two answers, we discuss as a class how many answers they need to choose. I often give them whiteboards to write down their answers before they try it on the computer. We also teach them to scroll for part B of a question, which many students initially overlook. This step-by-step guidance helps them feel more confident when they encounter similar tasks in future assessments.

The types of item frames we use depend entirely on students' needs. This school year, for instance, there's a heavy emphasis on literacy in my class, so I've created item frames based on what students still struggle with, such as CVC (consonant-vowel-consonant) words. I tailor these activities to reinforce what they've learned, especially if it's been a while since we covered the material.

Data notebooks are a key part of our process. Each student has a notebook with printed standards and proficiency scales. When they hit a target, they color it in and track their progress. Every week during DIBELS progress monitoring, they update their goals and see how they're progressing. This helps them reflect on what they've achieved and what they still need to work on, making them active participants in their learning. If they miss a goal, we revise their strategies, focusing on areas they can improve.

Grace Mussman
Grace Mussman is a fourth-grade teacher at Woodland Elementary School in Aurora, Colorado.

As I step into my fourth-grade classroom, I immediately feel a sense of belonging and comfort. I can't help but notice the pure joy I feel being in the classroom with my students. There's pride emanating from both my students and me, and excitement fills the room. My students are fully engaged in their learning, and my natural ability to spark and guide class discussions is immediately apparent. I strongly believe that students do their best when they have control over their own learning. For me, creating student choice and giving them a voice in the classroom are essential.

I strongly believe in making the classroom a home for students. This is where students spend their entire day. If students do not feel accepted, loved, and heard, then learning won't take place. However, once students know that they have a voice in the classroom, they feel loved and truly believe that their voice matters. This is when the learning will skyrocket. It is when you have created a comfortable, welcoming, and accepting classroom environment, where each student knows they are loved and cared about, that the learning becomes powerful. I believe that students know and feel when they are truly loved. Once you have created this positive environment for the students and they know how much you care, you are ready to blast off. Student voice and choice are powerful in the classroom. When students feel they are in charge of their own learning, this is when the real learning takes place. My job as an educator is to create a space for students to be able to thrive, learn, grow, explore, make connections, and make mistakes. Mistakes are also powerful and lead to nothing but greatness. You will immediately notice the level of comfort that not only the students have but I have as well. The way students dive into the content and feel comfortable sharing their ideas paints a clear picture of the accepting classroom environment where all students' voices matter and are heard.

I have a special way of doing guided discourse in my classroom. I run my class discussions in a way that captures all student voices, makes the learning engaging, and has students walking away feeling successful. As we know, all students learn differently. It is important to know each student's learning style and proficiency level. For example, let's say there is a student who is not quite on grade level, but nobody except the teacher knows that. It is crucial that, in order for that student to feel successful, the entire class hear and highlight this student's accomplishments and new discoveries. This gives the student a voice during the lesson. It also shows other students that this student was able to share and make a connection with the learning. It allows other students to make connections based on their unique and individual learning discoveries. It is important to give all students an opportunity to feel successful in their learning.

Let's take a look at a different example. Let's say this student is above grade level, but it is important to give them a voice and allow them to feel like a leader, as they are able to grasp the content quickly. By allowing this student to share their discoveries and ideas, I give them the opportunity to feel proud of their quick thinking, and other students can make immediate connections as they hear student voices do the teaching, rather than just me. Once a few students have discovered the correct answer as I walk around, I allow those students to go check other students' work. It is amazing how much students enjoy checking work and helping their classmates. They not only feel a sense of leadership when teaching but also provide student-to-student feedback immediately.

To probe students' thinking, I will teach a quick concept, then let students know they have a set amount of time to explore and practice the skill before sharing ideas. This allows students independent and hands-on learning directly after my minilesson. As I walk around, I confer with as many students as possible. This provides one-on-one coaching and immediate feedback. Students then take that coaching moment and immediate feedback and apply them to their learning. As I walk around during the lesson, I notice that multiple students have made a similar error. This is a perfect opportunity for "catch and release." This is a time for me to get the students' attention and provide clear additional instruction to help guide their learning. After I confer with as many students as possible and maximize independent learning time, at the end of the lesson, students can share what they learned or what they are proud of. Students just did a lot of independent learning. It is important to give them a voice and allow them to share what they are proud of in their learning. I allow students to form pairs or small groups and talk with each other. After a few minutes, I get the class's attention and allow students to share with the entire class. It is a beautiful moment to see students sharing their learning discoveries and being proud of themselves.

Another important aspect of student voice is treating students with respect, not like they are beneath you or less knowledgeable or wise than you. I make sure my students know that they matter, they are important, and I want to hear everything they have to say. This encourages students to truly open up and share their thoughts. Student growth and achievement happen when students feel comfortable in the classroom and have choices in their learning. Here's an example: I might give students the option to either edit their opinion-writing paragraph or continue to brainstorm another day. Both of these options are great and on topic with what we are learning. Once you give the students the choice, they immediately feel they are in charge of their learning and have a sense of independence and ownership in their work.

When calling on a student, I always repeat what that student said. This allows the student's voice to be a significant part of the learning. Each student has a second opportunity to hear their classmates' connections to the learning. I will then ask a different student to build on the previous student's answer. This immediately allows students who may have a similar answer but are reluctant to share feel they can build on the previous student's answer to create a chain of discovery.

The goal in my classroom is to get as many student voices heard as possible. I do this by probing students' thinking. I make it very clear to my students that their voices matter and are meaningful in any class discussion. It is important to allow students time to form connections to and make new discoveries about the content that was just taught. I have students share their thoughts in small groups, creating more voice for students. This removes the pressure for students who are worried their thinking is incorrect or are apprehensive about sharing with the whole class. The more voices heard—and the louder the classroom gets—the better. It is amazing to hear students share, debate, and collaborate during this time. As this is happening, I walk around the classroom and listen for key words from each small group. I then say, "Thirty more seconds." This allows students to wrap up their thinking and share their final thoughts. I ring the chime, signaling it's sharing time. It is exciting to see how many students want to contribute to the discussion using this strategy. Class discussions can and should be stimulating and spark growth for both learners and educators. Engaging class discussions capture a wide variety of student voices rather than only those of the first one or two students who raise their hands. In just a short time, nearly every student's voice is heard as they connect and collaborate.

It is critical that students confidently own their voices. Students are eager to expand their learning, and teachers must create opportunities for them to thrive and grow. Teachers have the responsibility to motivate students to excel. An environment where students are loved and valued produces confident learners. This passion for learning creates a clear path to student achievement and leadership. Now, the learning is unstoppable and truly becomes magic.

SUMMARY

This chapter dealt with four instructional practices that support the use of item frames in the classroom: (1) cumulative review (students continually reviewing and updating their knowledge of content previously addressed), (2) journaling (students keeping a running record of their understanding of content and the changes they have made to their understanding), (3) questioning techniques (teachers making questions more rigorous by organizing them around item types), and (4) guided discourse (teachers probing students' thinking, identifying insights and misconceptions, and asking students to reflect on their thinking). We also introduced a process we refer to as the *successive relearning instructional cycle*, which starts with the identification of key topics that will be addressed throughout the school year and then employs cumulative review, journaling, questioning techniques, and guided discourse in an integrated fashion. This chapter ended with examples of how classroom teachers adapt these instructional practices to meet the specific needs of their students. This chapter provided concrete examples of the various ways teachers might use item frames in their classrooms. In effect, item frames are not an anomaly to be employed only before important tests. Rather, the logic behind test-specific thinking can be incorporated into a wide variety of typical classroom activities.

CHAPTER 7

LEADING ITEM-FRAME USAGE AT THE SCHOOL AND DISTRICT LEVELS

Implementing new initiatives in schools, such as teaching test-specific thinking through item frames, requires intentional planning at the leadership level. This leadership can be district based or school based. This chapter addresses those issues as well as events leaders should plan for and ensure are enacted well. Specific issues and events include forestalling the criticism of "teaching to the test," understanding the limitations of external tests, interpreting students' scores on large-scale assessments, and initiating various school- and districtwide efforts. In addition, this chapter provides examples of how these initiatives might manifest in the field.

MISCONCEPTIONS ABOUT *TEACHING TO THE TEST*

Relative to implementing a schoolwide initiative regarding item frames, one of the first things leaders should address is the concept of teaching to the test. *Teaching to the test* is a phrase that is ubiquitous in education but often misused, and even more often misunderstood. It is certainly true that some—perhaps many—teachers, parents, and community members will have the initial reaction that the use of item frames is teaching to the test, and this is not something that schools should do. It is best to take on this perspective right from the start of the initiative.

Researchers and theorists who design tests have a great many recommendations on this topic. As summarized by Robert J. Marzano, Christopher W. Dodson, Julia A. Simms, and Jacob P. Wipf (2022), the literature on testing typically identifies three forms of teaching to the test, or *test preparation* (to use the more formal term): (1) instruction in the relevant subject matter, (2) test familiarization, and

(3) test-taking tricks. The first two types are not only legitimate but also necessary for a school to provide for its students.

The first type of test preparation, instruction in the relevant subject matter, involves ensuring that students have an opportunity to learn the content on which they are to be tested. Schools tend to prepare students in this way by making sure they are taught the content in their state standards. Since state-level tests are typically based on state standards documents, schools assume that teaching the standards adequately prepares students for state tests.

The second type of test preparation, test familiarization, involves exposing students to the general processes involved in test taking, familiarizing them with different item formats, and teaching basic strategies for approaching different types of items. This second type of test preparation is the focus of this book, with a special emphasis on item types and strategies for approaching various types of items.

The third type of test preparation, test-taking tricks, involves strategies designed to exploit flaws in the test design or individual items. For example, this type of test preparation involves teaching students strategies to enhance the probability of correctly answering a multiple-choice question for which they do not know the answer. This type of test preparation not only does not help students develop their understanding of content or their critical-thinking skills but also invalidates the information provided in the test for those students who are using these strategies (Haladyna, 2016).

Despite the general perspective from some educators that testing companies frown on any type of test preparation, there is considerable support for the first two types described here. For example, Thomas M. Haladyna and Steven M. Downing (2004) noted that "all students should receive ethical test preparation and the extensiveness of this ethical test preparation should be uniform" (p. 21), and College Board (2023) advised students that "the more you practice, the more familiar you'll be with the test format and content on test day."

Probably the strongest recommendations from testing experts regarding test preparation can be found in the technical literature on construct-irrelevant variance. As introduced in chapter 1 (page 3), *construct-irrelevant variance* refers to the differences in students' scores (that is, the variance) that can be caused by aspects of a test that have nothing to do with students' knowledge of the content. Charles DePascale and Brian Gong (2020) explained construct-irrelevant variance this way:

> If two students have equal levels of content knowledge and skills but differ in their familiarity with the item formats and tools used in the assessment, it is likely that the student who is more familiar and comfortable with the assessment will earn a higher test score. The observed difference in student performance would be

attributed to construct-irrelevant variance (i.e., familiarity with the assessment). (p. 41)

The technical manual for test designers is the book *Standards for Educational and Psychological Testing* (American Educational Research Association, American Psychological Association, & National Council on Measurement in Education [AERA, APA, & NCME], 2014). Standard 6.5 in this manual specifically addresses construct-irrelevant variance: "Test takers should be provided appropriate instructions, practice, and other support necessary to reduce construct-irrelevant variance" (AERA, APA, & NCME, 2014, p. 116).

Standard 4.16 elaborates on the type of preparation students should receive:

> The instructions presented to test takers should contain sufficient detail so that test takers can respond to a task in the manner that the test developer intended. When appropriate, sample materials, practice or sample questions, criteria for scoring, and a representative item identified with each item format or major area in the test's classification or domain should be provided to the test takers prior to the administration of the test, or should be included in the testing material as part of the standard administration instructions. (AERA, APA, & NCME, 2014, p. 90)

Finally, standard 8.2 broadens the scope of recommendations involving test preparation even further:

> Test takers should be provided in advance with as much information about the test, the testing process, the intended test use, test scoring criteria, testing policy, availability of accommodations, and confidentiality protection as is consistent with obtaining valid responses and making appropriate interpretations of test scores. (AERA, APA, & NCME, 2014, p. 134)

From these standards and the discussion before them, it seems eminently clear that testing experts not only support appropriate test preparation but consider it a necessary activity if students are to be fairly assessed on their knowledge of specific subject areas. Understanding the precise test-specific thinking that is required to correctly answer some types of items is one of the more important aspects of ethical test preparation.

THE LIMITATIONS OF EXTERNAL TESTS

In addition to informing their constituents about the strong support for ethical test preparation, school leaders should help educators and noneducators understand the nature and limitations of large-scale assessments like state tests. Underlying the belief that any type of test preparation is a form of cheating is the belief that large-scale assessments like state tests are pure and accurate measures of what students know and are able to do in various academic subject areas. Such a belief is founded on a number of fallacies people have long held about large-scale assessments. In general, there are three fallacies many educators and noneducators harbor about large-scale assessments.

1. A large-scale assessment measures all the important content in a given subject area.
2. A large-scale assessment is a highly accurate measure of a student's knowledge of a given subject area.
3. If students know the content on a large-scale assessment, they will be able to correctly answer the items on the test.

We debunk these misconceptions in the following sections.

Fallacy 1: A Large-Scale Assessment Measures All the Important Content in a Given Subject Area

One fallacy about large-scale assessments is that they address all the important content in a given subject area (Marzano, Warrick, & Acosta, 2024). At first blush, this seems to make sense. After all, the source of the content addressed in a large-scale assessment designed by an external testing company is the standards documents for the state. It makes sense that testing companies would consult these documents when designing tests for a particular state; as long as they design items based on the content in the state documents, they can be sure teachers have taught the content and students have had a chance to learn the content. Unfortunately, this rather straightforward scenario unravels quickly when one examines state standards documents.

State standards documents—although useful for providing general goals for districts, schools, and teachers in terms of curriculum, instruction, and assessment within a given subject area—simply are not designed in such a way that they can be directly translated into reliable and valid tests. Indeed, they inherently contain many obstacles to effective test construction. Here, we summarize a few of those obstacles, as described in the book *Five Big Ideas for Leading a High Reliability School* (Marzano et al., 2024).

One obstacle is too much content. Robert J. Marzano, Philip B. Warrick, and Mario I. Acosta (2024) illustrated the problem of too much content using the mathematics standard, "Understands the properties of operations with rational numbers (e.g., distributive property, commutative and associative properties of addition and multiplication, inverse properties, identity properties)" (p. 30).

When you decompose or unpack this standard, at least five topics emerge.

1. Understanding the distributive property with rational numbers
2. Understanding the commutative property of addition with rational numbers
3. Understanding the commutative property of multiplication with rational numbers
4. Understanding the inverse property of rational numbers
5. Understanding the identity properties of rational numbers

This pattern can be found in the standards for virtually every subject area. To illustrate, after a thorough analysis of the Common Core standards, Robert J. Marzano, David C. Yanoski, Jan K. Hoegh, and Julia A. Simms (2013) identified seventy-three standards (which they refer to as *elements*) for eighth-grade ELA. They found an average of five topics per standard. An average of five topics embedded in each element translates to an eighth-grade ELA teacher being responsible for 365 topics in a single 180-day school year.

Another problem with standards is that they can be highly equivocal. To illustrate, consider the following fourth-grade mathematics standard (NGA & CCSSO, 2010b): "Solve multistep word problems posed with whole numbers and having whole-number answers using the four operations [addition, subtraction, multiplication, and division], including problems in which remainders must be interpreted" (4.OA.A.3).

Marzano and colleagues (2019) explained that it is clear that the overall focus of this standard is multistep problems with whole numbers and whole-number answers. But this statement represents a huge range of possibilities. A given problem designed from this standard could involve any combination of the four basic operations and any combination of steps required to solve the problem. This level of variability makes it almost impossible to ensure that students are adequately taught the content to prepare them well, even for this one standard.

Because of the large amount of content in state standards and the ambiguity and redundancy in those standards documents, test makers have no choice but to sample the content and then build items around those samples. This practice is referred to as *domain sampling*. It involves the following components.

1. **Define the domain:** The first step is to clearly define the domain, which could be a body of knowledge (like algebra) or a set of skills (like reading comprehension). This involves identifying the key concepts, skills, or knowledge areas that the test is intended to assess.
2. **Determine test specifications:** Test makers create a blueprint or set of specifications for the test, outlining what proportion of the test will

cover each part of the domain. For example, in a mathematics test, 30 percent might be allocated to algebra, 20 percent to geometry, and so on.

3. **Select a representative sample:** Items (questions) are then selected from the larger domain for inclusion on the test. The goal is to choose items that collectively represent the domain as a whole. This process is similar to how a pollster might select a sample of voters to predict the outcome of an election.

4. **Construct and review items:** The selected items are constructed, reviewed, and often tested in pilot studies to ensure they accurately measure the intended content or skills. This step helps ensure that the sample of items is both representative of the domain and fair to test takers.

5. **Assemble the test:** Once the items are validated, they are assembled into the final test. The test is designed to cover the domain adequately, with the understanding that it cannot assess every single aspect of the domain—rather, it provides a snapshot of a test taker's knowledge or abilities in that domain.

If a test maker is creating a reading comprehension test for fourth graders, the domain might include skills like identifying the main idea, making inferences, and understanding vocabulary. Instead of testing every possible passage and question type, the test maker chooses a set of passages and questions that are representative of those skills. The goal is for the test results to reflect the student's overall reading comprehension ability, based on how they perform on this selected sample of items.

The process of domain sampling exacerbates the problem of too much content and sets up a *hit or miss* phenomenon in schools relative to what students are taught versus what they are tested on. The teachers in a school might be teaching selected content in their state standards effectively, but if that content is not what appears on the state test, their students might do poorly on the test, even though they learned the content that was directly taught to them.

In conclusion, the fallacy that large-scale assessments measure all the important content in a given subject area should be replaced with the generalization that large-scale assessments measure only a sampling of the content found in standards documents for specific content areas.

Fallacy 2: A Large-Scale Assessment Is a Highly Accurate Measure of a Student's Knowledge of a Given Subject Area

Another common fallacy about large-scale assessments is that they are highly accurate ways to measure an individual student's knowledge of a subject area. This fallacy can be demonstrated by the psychometric concept of *standard error of measurement* (SEM), a straightforward concept that can be understood at an intuitive level. Technical articles on its calculation are available from a simple internet search (for example, see www.statology.org/standard-error-of-measurement). Briefly, though, all assessments, no matter how well constructed, contain error. Test designers estimate the amount of error one can expect in a single student's score by computing the SEM. The standard error is the typical amount of inaccuracies you can expect in any individual student's score at any given point in time. The measurement is dependent on the standard deviation of a test and the reliability of the test. The formula for the standard error of measurement is the standard deviation times the square root of 1 minus the reliability.

Standard error of measurement =
standard deviation × square root of (1 − the reliability)

To illustrate, if a test has a standard deviation of 8 and a reliability of 0.95, the SEM is 1.79. In contrast, if a test has a standard deviation of 8 and a reliability of 0.80, the SEM is 3.58. As these examples illustrate, as the reliability of a test gets lower, the standard error of measurement gets bigger.

One way to demonstrate the amount of error surrounding an individual student's score is to calculate the 68 percent confidence interval (CI) around an individual score. The *68 percent confidence interval* is the range of scores within which one can be 68 percent sure that the student's true score falls. The 68 percent confidence interval is determined by adding and subtracting one standard error around the student's obtained score. This is depicted in figure 7.1 (page 108) for a student's score of 75 on a test that has a standard deviation of 8. For comparison's sake, the figure depicts the 68 percent confidence interval for the score of 75 across four levels of reliability: 0.80, 0.85, 0.90, and 0.95. This is a fairly wide range in terms of reliability coefficients, but it is instructive to note that all four of these reliabilities would be considered acceptable for a large-scale assessment (Rosaroso, 2015).

The 68 percent confidence interval for a score of 75 is between 73.21 and 76.79 when the reliability of the test is 0.95. However, that confidence interval widens, with a range from 71.42 to 78.58, when the reliability drops to 0.80. In other words, if a student scores a 75 on a test, the range of scores within which you can be 68 percent confident that the student's true score falls is quite large, even when the test has a relatively high reliability.

Similarly, the *95 percent confidence interval* is the range of scores within which you can be 95 percent sure (that is, confident) the student's true score lies. Figure 7.2 (page 109) depicts this confidence interval across four levels of reliability.

When the test has a reliability of 0.95, you can be 95 percent sure that the student's true score falls somewhere between 71.49 and 78.51. However, if the test has a reliability of 0.80, you can be 95 percent sure the student's true score falls somewhere between 67.99 and 82.01.

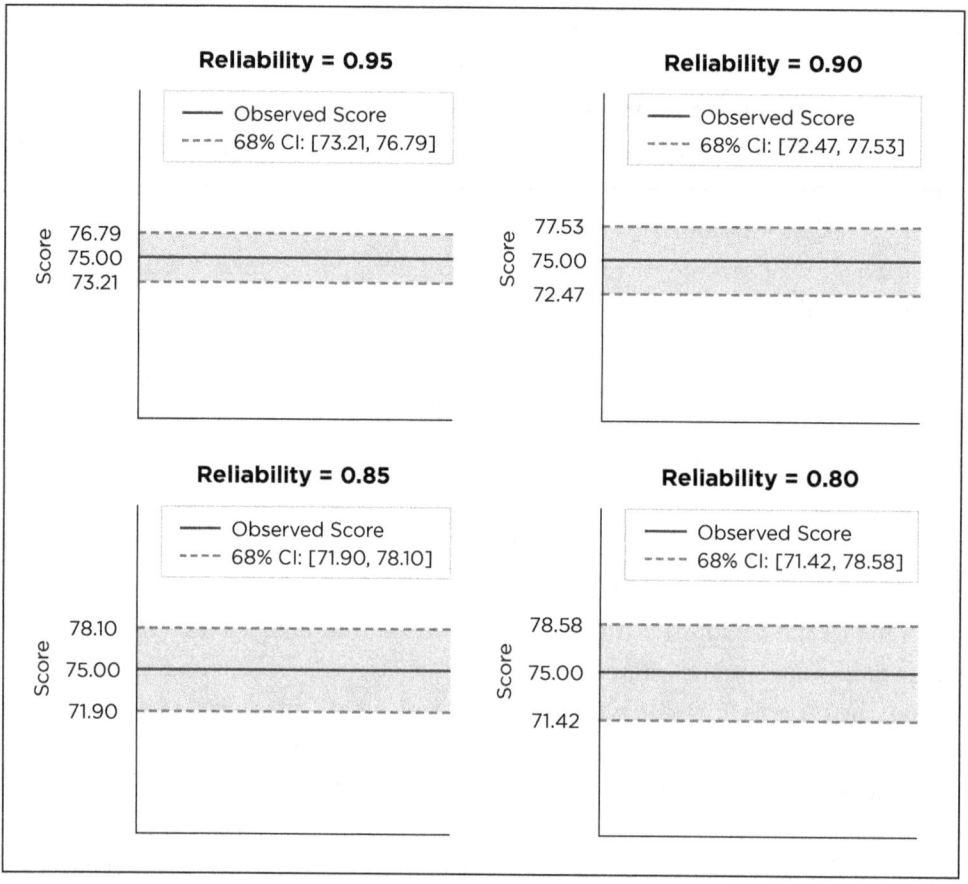

FIGURE 7.1: The 68 percent confidence interval.

All of these confidence intervals indicate substantive error in the scores reported for an individual student. What is probably most shocking to classroom educators is that even when a test has high reliability, like 0.95, the 68 percent confidence interval is 73.21 to 76.79, and the 95 percent confidence interval is 71.49 to 78.51. Stated in very concrete terms, even when a test has extremely high reliability, like 0.95, you can never say with absolute certainty that the score assigned to an individual student actually represents the true score for that student. Again, even though a student received a score of 75 on a test, you must assume that the student's true score could be as high as 78.51 or as low as 71.49 if you want to be 95 percent sure of your judgment about the student's true status.

Even the largest and most consequential tests hold this same pattern of uncertainty. The SEM of the SAT is about 30 points for mathematics, evidence-based reading, and writing (College Board, 2018). The typical SEM for the ACT is 2 to 3 points for each of the four sections: English, mathematics, reading, and science (ACT, 2024).

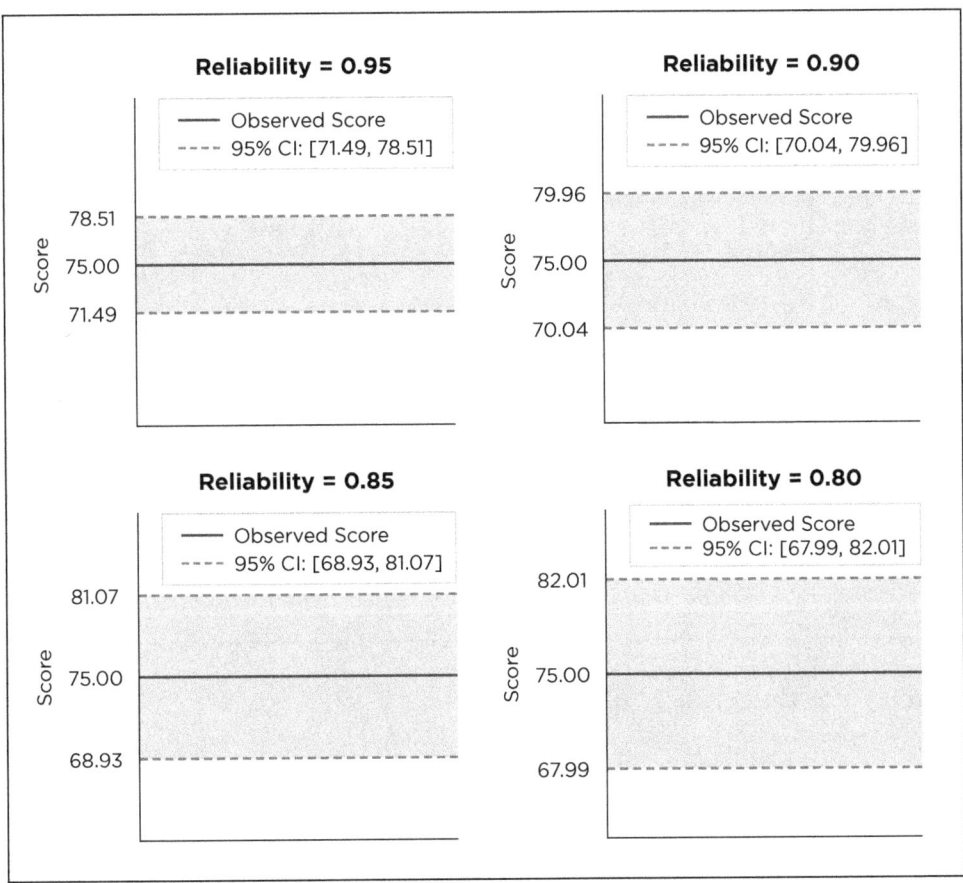

FIGURE 7.2: The 95 percent confidence interval.

In conclusion, the fallacy that a large-scale assessment is a highly accurate measure of a student's knowledge of a given subject area should be replaced with the generalization that large-scale assessments provide useful information about an individual student's knowledge at a given point in time, but that individual score should never be considered sufficient evidence to make academic decisions about that student.

Fallacy 3: If Students Know the Content on a Large-Scale Assessment, They Will Be Able to Correctly Answer the Items on the Test

The third fallacy surrounding large-scale assessments is that items on these assessments are designed in such a way that if students know the content being assessed, they will be able to correctly answer the items. Of course, this fallacy is the centerpiece of this book. As multiple examples in previous chapters have demonstrated, the test items themselves can provide obstacles for students answering them correctly, even when they know the content. For emphasis, we offer one final example of this phenomenon. Consider the fifth-grade mathematics item in figure 7.3 (page 110).

The table shows the beam diameter of four lasers.

Laser	Beam Diameter (meters)
Beam 1	0.0016
Beam 2	0.0008
Beam 3	0.0045
Beam 4	0.0020

Fill in the empty boxes with the symbols and numbers below to create correct comparisons. Use each number and symbol no more than once.

| 0.0008 | 0.0045 | > | = | < |

0.0016 ___ ___   0.0020 ___ ___
     Comparison 1   Comparison 2

Source: Marzano, Dodson, et al., 2022, p. 225.
FIGURE 7.3: Fifth-grade mathematics item.

This problem presents students with four lasers, and each laser has a beam diameter measured in meters. Ostensibly, students are asked to compare the beam diameters of these lasers using the symbols < (less than), > (greater than), and = (equal to). On the surface, the problem looks fairly straightforward. The beams have the following diameters.

- Beam 1: 0.0016 meters
- Beam 2: 0.0008 meters
- Beam 3: 0.0045 meters
- Beam 4: 0.0020 meters

Most fifth-grade students could probably rank the order of the lasers quite easily in terms of their diameters.

- 0.0008 (beam 2)
- 0.0016 (beam 1)
- 0.0020 (beam 4)
- 0.0045 (beam 3)

Fifth-graders could also easily use appropriate symbols to represent relationships, like the following.

- 0.0016 > 0.0008
- 0.0008 < 0.0045

But the problem requires students to use the numbers and symbols in a specific and unusual way. The problem provides students with two comparisons to complete, with one number already identified in each comparison. Comparison 1 has the number 0.0016 filled in on the left and an empty box for the second number on the right. Comparison 2 has the number 0.0020 filled in on the left and an empty box for the second number on the right. Given that two numbers are already filled in for each comparison, there are only two numbers left to fill in: the second number on the right in both comparisons. Those numbers are 0.0008 and 0.0045. This is a highly contrived situation and would rarely, if ever, occur in a context other than a test. As it turns out, there are two possible ways to solve the problem.

Consider comparison 1, which already has the number 0.0016 filled in on the left. If a student puts the number 0.0008 in the second box on the right, then the comparison symbol the student must use is > because 0.0016 is greater than 0.0008. This leaves only one number for the second comparison, and that number is 0.0045. So, the two numbers in comparison 2 would be 0.0020 on the left and 0.0045 on the right. The comparison symbol would be < because 0.0020 is less than 0.0045. This works because the student hasn't used the less-than sign yet. Finally, the equal sign isn't used at all.

But the problems can also be solved in a different way. In comparison 1, 0.0016 was already filled in. Suppose the student puts 0.0045 in the second box. The student would then have to use the symbol < because 0.0016 is less than 0.0045. This leaves the student with one number, 0.0008, and one sign, >, and the relations in the second comparison would be 0.0020 is greater than 0.0008. This works also. Again, the equal sign isn't used.

The type of thinking necessary to solve this problem is complex, and there is certainly nothing wrong with asking students to engage in complex reasoning. But the item purports to measure students' abilities to identify the relationships of *less than*, *greater than*, and *equal to* and use the appropriate symbols to signify these relationships. Even a student who previously learned these relationships and symbols may not answer the problem correctly simply because of the unrelated complex thinking it requires.

Test-specific thinking like this occurs in many forms. As we saw in the chapters regarding ELA, items that supposedly require students to determine the main idea of a passage commonly require students to examine and evaluate main ideas generated by test makers and then support those ideas with evidence from the text. As we saw in the chapters regarding mathematics, items that supposedly require students to demonstrate rather simple operations involving addition, subtraction, multiplication, and division commonly require students to first unravel a complex set of relationships between categories of persons, places, or things that would never be required of students outside of a testing situation.

It is also important to note that the very fact that test items use a multiple-choice format introduces an artificial type of thinking during a testing situation. This type of thinking is almost never required outside of a testing situation. Finally, even the fact that large-scale assessments are timed imposes an artificial constraint on students' thinking during the administration of the test.

In conclusion, the fallacy that as long as students know the content on a large-scale assessment, they will be able to correctly answer the items on the test should be replaced with the generalization that students might know the content on test items but still answer those items incorrectly because they haven't been prepared for the test-specific thinking inherent in the test.

INTERPRETATION OF A STUDENT'S SCORE ON A LARGE-SCALE ASSESSMENT

Given the weaknesses and flaws of large-scale assessments, a reasonable question educators and noneducators might ask is, "How do we interpret a student's score on a large-scale assessment?" The answer to this question is different depending on whether the student receives a high score or a low score.

If a student receives a low score on a large-scale assessment, there are a number of possible reasons why, including the following.

- The student did not learn the content assessed in the large-scale assessment because the school curriculum did not cover the content assessed.
- The school curriculum addressed the content on the large-scale assessment, but the student did not learn it.
- The student learned the content on the large-scale assessment either in school or outside of school, but the student was not prepared for the test-specific thinking required to answer the test items.
- The student learned the content on the large-scale assessment, but because of the inherent error in all tests, the student's score on the test was lower than the score the student would have received if that error had not been present.

If a student receives a high score on a large-scale assessment, there are a number of possible reasons why, including the following.

- The school curriculum did not cover the content on the large-scale assessment, but the student learned the content on the assessment outside of the school environment.
- The student learned the content on the large-scale assessment because that content was addressed in the school curriculum.

- The student learned the content on the large-scale assessment and was prepared for the test-specific thinking required by the test.
- The student learned the content on the large-scale assessment, and the inherent error in all tests did not adversely affect the student's score.

While a school cannot address all factors that would produce an artificially low score for a student on a large-scale assessment, it is clear from the preceding scenarios that a school can and should ensure that (1) the content on the large-scale assessment is part of the taught curriculum in the school, and (2) all students are prepared for test-specific thinking. Recall from the discussion earlier in the chapter that these two actions represent the two types of ethical test preparation recommended by testing experts.

SCHOOLWIDE INITIATIVES

There are a number of implications for schoolwide initiatives that emerge as a result of a greater awareness about the weaknesses of large-scale assessments. Here, we discuss a few.

Start an Assessment-Literacy Campaign

One somewhat obvious implication of the information about large-scale assessments discussed thus far is that the information presented in this book and others like it should be passed on to all teachers, parents and guardians, and other important constituent groups such as district board members. Such information might be presented in the context of an assessment-literacy initiative. The purpose of an assessment-literacy initiative should be to communicate the following facts about large-scale assessments.

- They are part of the culture of K–12 education.
- They do not measure all the important content that is taught in school.
- The scores they produce are not necessarily accurate for individual students.
- Students might know the content on a large-scale assessment but answer some items incorrectly because of the nature of the items themselves.
- They are used in the vast majority of professions students will aspire to once they matriculate from the K–12 education system.
- Even though they are imperfect instruments, they will probably be part of every student's life, even after school.

To make these points, the assessment-literacy initiative should present factual information, such as the shortcomings of standards, the error disclosed by the SEM, and so on. Books like *Making Classroom Assessments Reliable and Valid* (Marzano, 2018) and *The New Art and Science of Classroom Assessment* (Marzano et al., 2019) are good sources for such information.

An assessment-literacy campaign can take a number of forms. One of the easiest to develop and execute is video-recorded presentations to parents, guardians, and community members about the nature of large-scale assessments and how they should be interpreted.

Send Item Frames Home

It is imperative to have parents and guardians involved as much as possible in a school or district test-specific thinking initiative. Relative to item frames, the first step is to address the issue of teaching to the test. The assessment-literacy initiative, as described in the previous section, should go a long way toward addressing this issue.

Once the teaching-to-the-test issue has received adequate attention, we recommend the school identify strategies that can be used at home for various item frames and ensure that these home-based activities are coordinated across the entire school or district. For instance, a school might distribute a big idea scavenger hunt worksheet on a Friday. Over the next week, students and their families could identify the main idea in various contexts, such as in movies they watched over the weekend or in dinner-table conversations. Families might have a means to record these discussions and could possibly be motivated by incentives, like a pizza party for the classroom that produces the best scavenger hunt results at the end of the month or quarter. When families actively participate in item-frame discussions at home, it helps ensure students internalize the concepts more deeply, enhancing their understanding of how best to master test-specific thinking.

Another option is to provide training for parents and guardians on the nature and possible use of item frames at home. Principal Teolyn Bourbonnie and instructional coach Julie Mueller of Woodland Elementary School in Colorado sent a packet home to all parents regarding item frames and then held a Zoom-based training for parents who wished to understand item frames and learn how to use them to help their children develop test-specific thinking skills. Parents who attended were highly interested in the information they received about test-specific thinking and recognized its importance in the lives of their children.

Of course, a comprehensive home-based initiative would require addressing aspects like non-native English speakers at home, a lack of time in the home environment to support the use of item frames, a lack of understanding about the concept, and the like. These factors notwithstanding, it is perfectly legitimate to reach out to parents and guardians to at least inform them of such initiatives. Additionally, there are a growing number of resources for home-based item-frame instruction available that parents and guardians can use (such as Peak Curriculum; www.peakcurriculum.com).

Obtain Information From Students

To some extent, obtaining information from students about the item-frame initiative will happen automatically as students begin to learn more about item types. As principal of an elementary school that introduced item frames to students, Brian Kosena witnessed one class of students describing what they were learning about items as "breaking the code." More specifically, when students became aware that many test items have their own schemas that they must understand before they can correctly answer the item, the students announced that they were learning how to "break the code" that tells them what to do on specific items.

Another way to gather information from students is to periodically survey them on various aspects of their use of item frames. Figure 7.4 contains an example of such a survey. Surveys allow students to reflect on their learning while providing insight for the teacher. Comparing student surveys allows the teacher to identify next steps. If 70 percent of students state that they have improved their assessment scores and their confidence with challenging questions, then the teacher can hold one-on-one conferences with the remaining 30 percent who feel differently and create a specific plan for supporting them.

Student Survey

1. On a scale of 1 to 5, have item frames helped you better understand challenging test questions (with *5* being a "Yes, definitely!" and *1* being a "Not at all")?

    1   2   3   4   5

2. What part of an item-frame lesson helps you the most?

    _____
    _____

3. What challenges (if any) are you experiencing when working on item-frame questions?

    _____
    _____

4. Do you have any suggestions or feedback for improving item-frame lessons?

    _____
    _____

FIGURE 7.4: Sample student survey questions.

Visit **MarzanoResources.com/reproducibles** *for a free reproducible version of this figure.*

To illustrate the types of results a survey can provide, consider table 7.1, which reports some of the results of a survey administered to 403 students at Westminster Public Schools in the early stages of their use of item frames.

TABLE 7.1: Results From Student Survey in Westminster Public Schools

STATEMENT	FAVORABLE RESPONSE	UNFAVORABLE RESPONSE
I found item frames useful for my learning.	75.1%	24.9%
After learning the item frames this year, I felt more prepared to answer questions on the state test.	73.1%	26.9%
After learning about item frames this year, I feel able to create my own items from the item frame.	55.4%	44.6%

Source: © 2023 by Westminster Public Schools. Used with permission.

The Westminster Public Schools survey also included open-ended questions that produced some positive responses from students, like the following.

- "Item frames made the state ELA test easier."
- "It helped me learn. Thank you."
- "It was fun."
- "It was fun, and I felt I could get a nice and good score."
- "Item frames really helped me a lot to understand and know how to answer the questions."
- "It was a challenge, but I enjoyed it."
- "My experience with item frames this year helped me during the state test because I remembered practicing them in literacy, so I was able to know what the question was asking."
- "They helped me out a lot."

It also produced some not-so-positive responses, like the following.

- "I did not like the item frames practice because it was really boring."
- "It was hard because sometimes, when I think I can't do it, I can't do it."
- "I hated it. I never want to see it again."
- "It didn't prepare us for the limited time that we had with the math test. During the math test, I felt really rushed and couldn't take my time on problems, much less check my work."

Analyze Student Errors

An additional step to student feedback is collecting data by analyzing student errors on item frames. This can be accomplished by looking at the results of an item-frame question and by talking with students. When a teacher simply scores questions on a test, they only find out who answered items correctly and who did not, with little or no information regarding why. However, analyzing broader patterns reveals key insights. If all students get a particular question wrong, that sends a message to the teacher that their instruction has gaps. For example, if all students are able to determine the main idea of a passage but many are unable to correctly provide evidence that supports their answer, the teacher knows that additional instruction on supporting evidence is required. A sample template of a tool to analyze student errors is found in figure 7.5.

Date: _____   Item frame: _____

Number of students: _____

Number of students who answered part A correctly: _____

Number of students who answered part B correctly: _____

Number of students who answered both part A and part B correctly: _____

Select two or three students who answered the item frame incorrectly and ask the following questions.

Can you explain what you thought the question was asking you?

What steps did you take to solve the problem or answer the question?

Can you pinpoint any mistakes you made or parts in the question that caused confusion?

FIGURE 7.5: Form to analyze student errors.

*Visit **MarzanoResources.com/reproducibles** for a free reproducible version of this figure.*

Use Classroom Observation to Provide Teachers With Feedback

Building item frames into a cycle of observation and coaching shows the staff that school leadership is committed to the initiative. When a principal observes item-frame instruction, it accentuates the message that this is something important to the success of the building. By following up with the teacher after the observation, the principal demonstrates that they are there to support and reflect with them.

In order to successfully create an observation cycle, teachers need to commit to a consistent time in their schedule each week to address item frames. For example, teachers might be given the task to do two item frames each week, one in ELA and one in mathematics. Teachers should have the flexibility to select the day of the week and the time of day in which a principal might observe them. Once a teacher has established their preferred day and time for observation, a principal can create an observation cycle. In the early stages, a principal should visit the teacher every other week. When observing, the principal should collect notes using an item-frame observation scale and an accompanying evidence chart like the ones in figure 7.6.

Within the first three weeks of implementation, we recommend devoting time in a staff meeting for teachers to discuss what is going well and what their needs are relative to item-frame usage. For example, the school leader might pose the following questions.

- What item frames have you experimented with so far in ELA and mathematics?
- What success have you seen among your students?
- What barriers or challenges are you experiencing?

By asking the first question, the principal is able to see which item frames teachers have been using across the building. It is also an opportunity for teachers to see what others are doing. One classroom teacher might initially be nervous about using the evidence frame but then hear from a colleague who has used it with success. This allows the reticent teacher to ask questions and seek advice from the teacher who has experienced success.

The second question allows staff to acknowledge and reflect on student success. It reminds classroom teachers that the purpose of item frames is to enhance student achievement and help students develop agency in testing situations.

The third question, regarding barriers and challenges, allows the principal to see what the needs are in the building. Are teachers having a hard time finding time in their schedules to do item-frame instruction? Are teachers unclear about how to analyze students' item-frame data? A principal can use this information to support the staff and plan professional development that is applicable to the challenge areas.

By the twelfth week of implementation, teachers should participate in data cycles with the instructional leaders in the building. These teams should include administrators, instructional coaches, or lead teachers or interventionists who can offer support. In these meetings, teachers bring all relevant data regarding their use of item frames and their effects on students. Open-ended questions are encouraged in these meetings to guide conversation. Questions that should be covered in these meetings include the following.

Implementation Goal: The teacher designs and implements item-frame questions that align with learning objectives. Students understand item frames and can identify and create their own item-frame questions.

Planning Question: What will I include in my lesson to teach the necessary vocabulary and content in order for students to complete item-frame questions successfully?

Teacher Evidence for Level 2 (Developing)	Student Evidence for Level 3 (Applying) or Level 4 (Innovating)
The teacher is: • Selecting or creating item frames that align with the lesson's objective • Finding grade-level (or scaffolded) resources that fit with the item frame • Identifying key vocabulary terms that require review or instruction • Teaching or reviewing necessary content • Modeling how to approach an item-frame question • Engaging students in guided questions to chunk the question and understand what is being asked • Informing students of the purpose of item frames and how they support learning	**The student is:** • Interacting with the learning and the required resources • Identifying which item frame is being used or taught • Identifying what the question is asking and steps to approach the question • Creating their own item-frame question when provided a sentence stem or example

	4 INNOVATING	3 APPLYING	2 DEVELOPING	1 BEGINNING	0 NOT USING
Item-Frame Rubric	The teacher engages in all behaviors at the Applying level. In addition, students are able to create their own item-frame questions with high rigor and identify the frame they selected and why.	The teacher engages in activities that teach students the required vocabulary and content without significant errors or omissions, and the majority of students understand item frames and their purposes. The teacher engages in guided discourse and cumulative review with the class.	The teacher uses item-frame questions without significant errors or omissions. Evidence for this level of performance includes (1) instruction on the vocabulary used in the item-frame question and (2) instruction on the content asked in the item-frame question.	The teacher uses item-frame questions but does so with errors or omissions, such as not instructing on the vocabulary or content required for the item.	The teacher does not use item frames.

FIGURE 7.6: Evidence chart and observation scale.

Visit MarzanoResources.com/reproducibles for a free reproducible version of this figure.

- How do you select which item frame to use? Are you finding one to be more successful than others? Do students prefer a particular frame?
- What information are you gaining from the use of item frames? Have you measured an increase in student achievement?
- Reflecting on your instruction with item frames, do you have any insights or other things you've noticed?

Seek Information From Teachers

For item frames to have their greatest impact on students, it is important to support teachers in reflecting on the success and inevitable challenges of this new initiative. Teachers should track which frames they utilize, how students respond to the frames, any errors that students make, and any findings that could drive the instructional planning for future item frames. Figure 7.7 provides an example of how a teacher can track their development in item frames.

Item-Frame Tracking

Following a lesson using item frames, take time to reflect and track your implementation. Use the item-frame teacher rubric (figure 7.6, page 119) as guidance.

Initial Score: _____   Goal Score: _____ by _____ (Date)

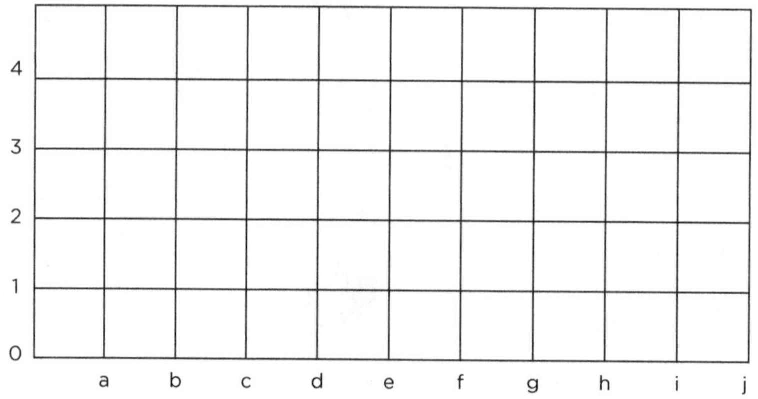

[Grid with y-axis values 0–4 and x-axis labels a through j]

Dates

a. _____   f. _____
b. _____   g. _____
c. _____   h. _____
d. _____   i. _____
e. _____   j. _____

FIGURE 7.7: Teacher reflection tool.

*Visit **MarzanoResources.com/reproducibles** for a free reproducible version of this figure.*

Note that this form refers to an item-frame rubric, as described in the previous section (see figure 7.6, page 119). After systematically tracking their progress, collaborative teams of teachers can debrief and identify common strengths and weaknesses. This can result in joint planning for how they might use particular item frames.

Encourage Collaboration and Co-Teaching

Team-based collaboration ensures that all teachers implement item frames consistently and offers opportunities for co-planning and co-teaching. A team-based approach offers some benefits. First, if teachers work together to identify their preferred methods for instruction, their use of item frames will ultimately lead to more effective and robust instruction. Additionally, teachers are more likely to adopt a new initiative when they have a say in the decision-making process as to how the initiative will be used. Finally, uniform implementation across teams allows school leaders to provide targeted feedback and more effectively monitor the rollout of the new initiative during their classroom observations, ultimately ensuring higher fidelity.

We recommend that each collaborative team set a specific day and time each week to focus on item frames. While item frames should be integrated into various lessons, having designated times for their use in subjects like ELA and mathematics can enhance consistency for both teachers and students. Establishing clear routines and procedures is crucial for successful implementation. For example, a teaching team might decide that item frames will be taught on Tuesdays and Thursdays during whole-group instruction. This could be followed by students applying what they've learned in a dedicated center during station rotations. The more precise the schedule for implementing item frames, the easier it will be for teachers and students to achieve success.

Co-teaching is a versatile and powerful approach used across various disciplines and for multiple purposes. When a principal actively engages teachers in co-teaching—especially with something specific, like item frames—they send a strong message about the initiative's importance to both teachers and students. The principal's involvement not only underscores the significance of the item frames but also helps shape the narrative around their use. For instance, if a principal describes item frames as tools for students to "crack the code" of testing and then participates in co-teaching sessions that demonstrate how to navigate different types of assessment challenges, they can make the implementation process seem more intriguing and directly relevant to students.

Monitor the Overall Effectiveness of the Item-Frame Initiative in the School

Ultimately, the success of an item-frame initiative is a function of how uniformly item frames are being used across a school and how observable their impact is. To this end, school leaders should continually monitor their item-frame initiatives using a performance scale like the one in figure 7.8 (page 122).

LEVEL	EVIDENCE
4 **Sustaining** **(Quick Data)**	Quick data like the following are systematically collected and reviewed. • Reviews of teachers' lesson plans and unit plans indicate continued effective use of item frames. • Walkthrough observation data indicate continued effective use of item frames. • Quick conversations with teachers and students indicate continued effective use of item frames.
3 **Applying** **(Lagging Indicator)**	• Concrete data indicate that students' performance on external tests has increased. • Ninety percent of teachers use item frames and can explain how and why they use them. • Observation data indicate that 90 percent of teachers systemically use item frames. • Ninety percent of teachers and 80 percent of students perceive item frames to be useful for their learning and their ability to do well on tests.
2 **Developing** **(Leading Indicator)**	• Teachers follow specific protocols for the use of item frames in their classrooms. • Item-frame usage is executed on a systematic basis according to schedule. • A walkthrough process is used to monitor the use of item frames in classrooms.
1 **Beginning**	• The school has written plans for the use of item frames, but there is no implementation at the school level. • While item frames are not used schoolwide, a few teachers utilize item frames in their classrooms.
0 **Not Using**	• The school has no written plans for the use of item frames. • There is no implementation of item frames at the classroom level.

Source: © 2020 by Marzano Academies, Inc. Adapted with permission.

FIGURE 7.8: Performance scale for determining school-level implementation of item frames.

This type of performance scale was introduced in the books *Leading a High Reliability School* (Marzano, Warrick, Rains, & DuFour, 2018) and *Leading a Competency-Based Elementary School* (Marzano & Kosena, 2022). School leaders should systematically assess their school's performance to ensure a continuous-improvement approach to item-frame use. At the not using level of the scale, the school has no written plans for the use of item frames or no use at the classroom level. At the beginning level, the school has written plans for item-frame use, but there is no implementation at the school level. At the developing level, item frames are being used throughout the building on a systematic and regular basis. The term *leading indicator* in the scale indicates that a specific program or practice is in place at an acceptable level. It is at the applying level of the scale that there is concrete evidence for the success of item frames. This evidence includes data on teachers' and students' perceptions as well as data regarding students' enhanced performance on tests. Data that indicate the programs and practices that are in place are producing the desired results are referred to as *lagging indicators*. Finally, at the sustaining level of the scale, quick data are collected continuously, and those data indicate that item-frame usage is strong and continuous. As the name implies, *quick data* are readily available or rather easily collected so that the effects of the programs and practices can be continuously monitored to ensure they are sustained.

ADAPTATIONS FROM THE FIELD

As was the case with classroom-level practices discussed in chapter 6 (page 89), leaders often adapt the school- and district-level activities discussed in this chapter for their unique situations. Here, we consider specific adaptations.

Mike Lynch

Mike Lynch is a district administrator in Westminster, Colorado, who has been with Westminster Public Schools since it started its competency-based initiative.

Although our approach was different from one school to another, one thing seemed present from the outset: We weren't sure what to call it, exactly, but it seemed like a combination of hesitation and resistance, and it sometimes invoked conversations that started like this.

- "I'm not sure teaching to the test is the solution to filling our achievement gaps."
- "What will I have to give up if I have to start using item frames?"
- "This feels like test prep, not authentic teaching."

But something else was present, too. This trend was not evident at first, but after a very short amount of time, we began to hear comments like this.

- "I wasn't sure how hard this would be, but after writing a few item frames and matching them to my proficiency scales, it actually became pretty easy."
- "We were slow to start, but once we got the hang of it, students were actually looking forward to working with item frames. They actually had fun eventually making their own!"

In addition to encouraging teachers to begin using item frames to help teach their content, we had two high school teams of three mathematics teachers and three ELA teachers meet after school each week to begin their construction of sample item frames based on the studies in *Ethical Test Preparation in the Classroom*. Over the course of about nine weeks, these two groups developed sample item frames with types consistent with those from the book and then were asked to reflect on their work with the following questions.

- What do you see from your item-frame-creation work now that you did not see when we first began our collaboration?
- What advice would you give your colleagues before they begin to leverage item frames as an instructional strategy?
- What insights would you give your students about working with item frames after the last three months of creating them?

Here's what one teacher had to say.

> We started the item-frame-creation process with the reaction that we were developing materials that would "teach to the test." This still holds true, but after going through the process of creating item frames, I see we have built an actionable resource that will allow more students to access success on standardized tests. The item frames present a structure that offers a way for students and teachers to build ownership of their learning.
>
> When sharing the concept of item-frame questions with other teachers, my advice would be to ask the questions, "What is working well now?" and "What are we not satisfied with in our own instruction and our students' learning?" Introducing item frames in this context will show that the frames can fill a need in the teaching-and-learning cycle. I believe students may be a harder sell. However, I would allow students to discover how powerful item frames can be by allowing them to see the difference in their mastery of a question or problem by comparing their work from before and after the item frame. As always, it would hinge on how well a teacher crafted this experience in the classroom.
>
> —*Jim Paris, secondary mathematics teacher*

Teachers at the Metropolitan Arts Academy in Westminster Public Schools were also at the forefront of utilizing item frames after a mid-year adjustment. They were asked the following questions.

- What did you learn from the process?
- Did anything surprise you?

Leading Item-Frame Usage at the School and District Levels

Here is how they responded.

I learned that students are much more adaptable and able to pick up on things once they are able to see things more transparently. Once they know the "formula" of how these item frames are written and the types that there are, students are able to quickly "plug in" the information and make it applicable to their own lives.

—**Dillon Lynch,** *middle school mathematics and science teacher*

What surprised me was the fun the kids had and the fun they had when they were writing these problems. I learned that my students can do these problems and have the ability to raise the bar.

—**Anthony Salazar,** *middle school mathematics teacher*

I learned that item frames aren't just about test prep! At first, I found them overwhelming, but I was excited as I became more comfortable with them. They were so easy to start to incorporate into every part of our day, across all content areas!

—**Dylan Shelofsky,** *level 5–6 teacher*

The students I worked with needed scaffolding, but they were very successful with support. I was surprised how quick students were to guess an answer versus go back and locate text evidence. We worked on this a lot.

—**Rachel Fox,** *Title I teacher*

We found that by incorporating visuals, thinking maps, sentence stems, and models, our English learners were able to understand the process more.

—**Sheila Romero,** *culturally and linguistically diverse teacher*

We found that English learners benefited from incorporating thinking maps, visuals, and sentences. This helped with their process of learning and targeted their specific learning needs.

—**Shannon Bowen,** *culturally and linguistically diverse teacher*

I knew that the vocabulary was going to be an important thing to learn before they started making their own questions and really working heavily with item frames, but I was surprised by how quickly the students were able to connect the questions to real-life scenarios. There were a few times when I found myself struggling to connect them, but the students weren't. That was really cool to see.

—**Andrea Howsden,** *special education teacher*

Lucy Pearson

Lucy Pearson is vice principal at John E. Flynn A Marzano Academy, in Westminster, Colorado.

While observing and coaching teachers regarding how to implement item frames, it quickly became clear to me that they understood them best when they began creating their own versions. If that is what benefited teachers the most and helped them make connections to proficiency scales, that is exactly what will happen if you start to have students creating their own items.

With the high school item-frame committee, the literacy teachers used the steps to create their own frames. Throughout this process, teachers recognized how important this work is. They started to analyze passages more, really pulling out what is important from the proficiency scales, and, most importantly, they began to recognize how confusing it can be for a student to answer questions on tests.

The biggest misconception we found regarding item-frame instruction is that teachers thought it was teaching to the test. We soon realized that, as educators, we have a set of content standards that we are required to teach our students. These standards include the expectation that students will master the content to such a degree that they pass on to the next grade level. This is our job. In our current educational system, student success is measured through standardized tests. If we know this, then it is our responsibility to teach students strategies that can support them when taking these big assessments. We know it is our duty to teach them the content—we already teach the important content in our standards documents. Why not use intentional instruction about testing formats when teaching that content?

Additionally, we soon realized that, as teachers, we can easily embed item-frame instruction into content instruction. And when we also use cumulative review, it's even better! Students (and people in general) are scared of the unknown. And a standardized test is often something that students fear. When we prepare our students and give them things to look for and identify in these high-stakes tests, it takes away the anxieties that often come with the daunting task of taking a test.

Another misconception that we initially heard from educators is that item-frame instruction takes away the creativity of a classroom. I think educators viewed it as a "drill-and-kill" type of method. We soon found that item-frame instruction can be highly engaging for students. Once students got used to them, they were intrigued by unlocking the complexity of the items. Teachers even found ways to make item-frame practice funny. For example, one ELA teacher introduced the big-idea item frame by using a passage about sewage. Within that passage, the word *poop* appeared many times, as well as other comical words that made the students giggle. In mathematics classes, teachers used "mystery mathematics," which involved game boards comprised of mystery-mathematics problems. Using mystery mathematics, students got to play a game while solving complex problems. We also found that students enjoyed it when they got to create their own frames. This is something they can easily do once they are familiar with the frames.

Claudette Trujillo
Claudette Trujillo is principal of the Metropolitan Arts Academy in Westminster, Colorado.

At the Metropolitan Arts Academy, we used the item-frame initiative as a way to increase the use of cognitively complex tasks—an area of growth our teachers identified in the Westminster Instructional Model, or WIM, as we call it.

Our first step was to have teachers review the various item frames to ensure they all shared a common understanding. Since the Metropolitan Arts Academy is a K–8 school, we organized separate teams for primary, intermediate, and secondary grade levels. Each team began by writing down what it already knew about item frames. Then, teams shared their responses with the other teams, comparing common understandings and misconceptions. To deepen their knowledge, all teams reviewed excerpts from the book *Ethical Test Preparation in the Classroom*. This helped them understand item frames in general as well as the types that specifically applied to their subject areas and grade levels.

After that, we moved on to application. We tasked the teams with crafting lessons that not only incorporated item frames but also addressed various question types. Our goal was to make these lessons engaging, inclusive, and tailored to our students' comprehension levels. In the classroom, teachers began by showing students how to decode different item types. They would identify what type of question it was and practice accordingly. For example, if it was a mathematics question, students worked on solving the equation with the teacher. If it was a reading question, students analyzed what the item was asking them to do based on the passage. Watching teachers break down and unpack items with students was incredibly powerful. Soon, we saw teachers and students making connections: Students said, "This sounds like the question from yesterday," and teachers said, "Even though it's different math we're doing, it's still written the same way."

We then shifted our focus to vocabulary. Teachers encouraged students to look for key words in each item to identify the type of question being asked. For a couple of weeks, this became a major focus, and during that time, teachers continually assessed how well students were understanding and applying item frames.

Eventually, we took the process a step further by having students write their own items. This turned out to be a game changer. The most exciting part for me was when we started goal setting, and students began incorporating item frames into their personal goals. We used a creative approach, which was fitting for an arts academy:

Students created self-portraits with speech bubbles that listed their three goals. Item frames frequently showed up in the intermediate grades because those students felt most successful. For example, students began writing goals like, "I can use item frames to help me solve difficult problems in mathematics." This shift demonstrated their ability to use item frames not just to practice decoding but also to showcase their learning.

The turning point came when students started taking pride in writing their own items and having them displayed in the hallways. Seeing their self-portraits alongside their goals, with language about item frames that they included naturally and without teacher prompting, was a clear sign of how meaningful and transformative this work had been. Students weren't just practicing cognitively complex tasks—they were mastering them and finding authentic ways to connect them to their learning.

Cindy Davis

Cindy Davis is principal of Sherrelwood Elementary School in Westminster, Colorado.

As the principal of Sherrelwood Elementary School, I've seen firsthand the transformative power of item frames in our classrooms. Our school, a competency-based elementary school, has made remarkable progress over time and was honored with a Bright Spot Award from Governor Jared Polis in 2022. I truly believe this success stems from the incredible dedication of our teachers and the implementation of item frames, which have helped our students develop critical thinking and master test-taking strategies tailored to different question types.

I first learned about item frames when another principal and I attended a training session with Bob Marzano. This was before the pandemic, probably the year before. During the session, Bob introduced us to the concept of item frames, and I was immediately intrigued. It wasn't that we hadn't been preparing our students for testing before; we had always provided them with support and strategies. But item frames offered something new—a way to refine and elevate our approach to test strategies.

Item frames are essential for teaching students to analyze questions, identify claims, and support those claims with evidence. After our training, about half of my staff gained a deeper understanding of this approach. We began exploring resources to find texts that aligned with specific teaching objectives, like identifying the point of view, understanding the author's purpose, or extracting big ideas.

Over time, our teaching methods evolved. We moved away from relying solely on textbook materials. Instead, our teachers became experts at selecting texts that matched their lessons' objectives. Whether it was teaching point of view or identifying the author's purpose, they chose passages that truly supported their goals. We introduced item-frame structures to our students as early as kindergarten, teaching them what to look for in texts. While whole-group instruction remained common, I found that the real magic happened in small groups. In those settings, students received focused support, starting with texts at their comprehension level and gradually advancing.

When it came to whole-class instruction, we incorporated item frames into activities like Kagan Structures. Teachers would often model the process, assigning heterogeneous groups to find evidence in various texts. Our students were already familiar with test formats like the AB structure, which made it easier for them to engage in these activities. Sometimes, each group analyzed a different passage, fostering diverse perspectives, while other times, the entire class worked on the same passage to encourage collaborative learning. Once the teacher modeled the process, the students took the lead in subsequent sessions, fostering both independence and critical thinking.

One of the most exciting aspects of item frames was empowering students to create their own. This was a true game changer. When students began designing their own item frames, they not only crafted questions but also created answer choices. This process required them to think critically and deeply about the material. In some classes, students even collaborated to create item frames for their peers, promoting peer-to-peer learning and collaboration. Encouraging students to take this active role shifted their focus from passively consuming information to actively constructing it. They learned to deconstruct texts, generate questions, and internalize the learning process.

And yes, students absolutely loved using item frames! They got a kick out of creating challenging questions and answers, and often included a silly option or subtle variations to make their questions more thought-provoking. Watching their enthusiasm and creativity was incredibly rewarding.

As for results, I've seen a profound impact on our students' ability to articulate their knowledge. Item frames have taught them how to structure their responses, enabling them to effectively demonstrate their understanding. This growth has been evident in various assessments, including CMAS, STAR, and teacher-made tests, where students consistently showcase their comprehension and analytical skills. Beyond being an instructional tool, item frames have become a means of assessment. They allow students to independently apply their learning, fostering accountability and ownership of their education.

In my opinion, item frames have truly transformed the way we teach and assess at Sherrelwood Elementary. The success we've achieved is a testament to the hard work of our teachers and the power of innovative teaching strategies.

Brenda Martin

Brenda Martin, now a district-level administrator, was the principal of Colorado STEM Academy in Westminster, Colorado.

One of the first things we like to do early in the school year is have teachers take a practice assessment. They log in and access online practice assessments that correspond to the subject they teach, whether it's ELA, mathematics, science, or another subject. They take the assessment from a teacher's perspective, giving them a chance to see what it looks like and to ensure their teaching aligns with that style.

We've conducted various trainings on incorporating item frames into instruction, but I think it's important for teachers to understand the reasoning behind this approach. It's just one part of teaching and learning, but it's a crucial one because it's how students are assessed. Ultimately, it comes down to professional development and collegial conversations about embedding these practices into our daily work.

Another key aspect is creating schoolwide systems to ensure these practices become part of our routine. For us, cumulative review fits perfectly into our early-release days. Teachers have time built in on Mondays to focus on this, and some, like Ms. Fritz, integrate it into their daily work. However, all our teachers incorporate it into their Monday schedules, which feature shorter class periods. This time is ideal for reinforcing knowledge through cumulative learning—practicing skills and incorporating item frames across all subjects, whether it's music, art, science, or social studies.

As an innovation school, we have early dismissal every Monday, giving us additional time with staff for professional development. On those days, we have six hours with students, and after they leave, we have two hours for staff development. Our early releases operate on a rotation, and part of this rotation is focusing on effective teaching, which includes embedding cumulative learning, revising knowledge, and using item frames. This training happens about once per month.

Our teachers, who are the experts, lead the training. They conduct the training, observe each other during instructional rounds, and bring their findings back to their teams. I firmly believe that the expertise we need is already in our building, and our teachers are the ones leading the way.

We've been focusing on cumulative learning and item frames at the Colorado STEM Academy for about three years, which coincides with when our district began placing greater emphasis on them. We began exploring them more deeply through the Westminster Instructional Model. After the pandemic, we experienced a setback, but we recognized the need to reinforce this type of learning for our students, which led to strong growth in the following years.

If I were to advise a principal who is just starting to explore cumulative learning and item frames, I would emphasize the importance of professional development. It needs to be ongoing and reflective, much like what we do with students. Educators need opportunities to revise their understanding of cumulative learning, whether through reading, observation, or collaboration. Building item frames requires time and consistent effort; it can't be a one-off event. Just as students benefit from cumulative learning, so do the adults in the system.

For aspiring or newer principals looking to implement these practices, I'd suggest identifying the teachers in your building who are passionate and can serve as leaders. These experts are everywhere, and it's important to tap into their leadership both within and outside of the school. For example, just this past Monday, our teachers visited other schools in the district to observe different approaches to item frames and cumulative learning. Seeing these practices in action helps teachers understand the why behind them, and once they do, they're ready to fully engage.

SUMMARY

This chapter dealt with school and district initiatives related to item-frame usage. A major recommendation was that leaders address the issue of teaching to the test right from the beginning of any school- or districtwide project. Leaders should provide concrete information about three fallacies regarding large-scale assessments and the need for schools and districts to engage their students in ethical test preparation. Once the issue of teaching to the test has been dealt with adequately, a number of school- or districtwide initiatives—ranging from assessment-literacy campaigns to analysis of students' errors to monitoring the overall effectiveness of item-frame instruction—are possible. This chapter ended with examples of how school and district administrators started and nurtured item-frame initiatives in their schools and districts. To be successful, item-frame initiatives must be implemented schoolwide, or even districtwide. By definition, such comprehensive initiatives require leadership to focus on specific issues and events, as detailed in this chapter.

EPILOGUE
PULLING BACK THE CURTAIN

In the 1939 movie *The Wizard of Oz*, it took Dorothy, the Scarecrow, the Tin Man, and the Cowardly Lion a long time to realize that the Wizard in Emerald City was not the benevolent, all-powerful entity watching over the land that they thought him to be. Instead, when the quartet confronted the Wizard, they found an all-too-human being hiding behind a curtain, pretending to have powers he did not possess. To a great extent, this book is designed to help educators pull back a similar curtain, one that has hidden the true nature of large-scale assessments for decades. The disclosures for educators might be as disquieting as those Dorothy and her comrades faced. Large-scale assessments are not the all-powerful, benevolent measures that many think them to be. While they have their place in the grand scheme of K–12 education, they have rather serious flaws and weaknesses. However, just as the man behind the curtain in *The Wizard of Oz* was ultimately a benefit to Dorothy, the Scarecrow, the Tin Man, and the Cowardly Lion, so, too, can large-scale assessments play a positive role in the lives of students and teachers if we know how to use them the right way. This book is intended to be a major step in articulating that "right way."

REFERENCES AND RESOURCES

ACT. (2006). *Reading between the lines: What the ACT reveals about college readiness in reading.* Author. Accessed at www.act.org/content/dam/act/unsecured/documents/reading_report.pdf on April 22, 2020.

ACT. (2024, January). *ACT technical manual.* Author. Accessed at www.act.org/content/dam/act/unsecured/documents/ACT_Technical_Manual.pdf on November 4, 2024.

Æsop (n.d.). The wolf in sheep's clothing. In *The Æsop for children.* Accessed at https://read.gov/aesop/022.html on May 21, 2025.

Ainsworth, L., & Viegut, D. (2006). *Common formative assessments: How to connect standards-based instruction and assessment.* Corwin Press.

American Educational Research Association, American Psychological Association, & National Council on Measurement in Education. (2014). *Standards for educational and psychological testing.* Authors. Accessed at www.testingstandards.net/uploads/7/6/6/4/76643089/standards_2014edition.pdf on November 5, 2024.

AVID Open Access. (n.d.). *Establish an engaging and sustained digital focused note-taking process.* Accessed at https://avidopenaccess.org/resource/digital-focused-note-taking-establish-an-engaging-sustained-process on September 1, 2024.

Bangert-Drowns, R. L., Hurley, M. M., & Wilkinson, B. (2004). The effects of school-based writing-to-learn interventions on academic achievement: A meta-analysis. *Review of Educational Research, 74*(1), 29–58.

Bradford, W. (1898). *Bradford's history "Of Plimoth Plantation."* Wright and Potter Printing Co. Accessed at www.gutenberg.org/files/24950/24950-h/24950-h.htm on May 21, 2025.

Brazil, A. (1914). *The youngest girl in the fifth* (S. Davis, Illus.). Blackie and Son.

Chatterjee, D., & Corral, J. (2017). How to write well-defined learning objectives. *The Journal of Education in Perioperative Medicine, 19*(4), Article E610.

College Board. (2018). *2018 SAT suite of assessments annual report: Total group*. Author. Accessed at https://reports.collegeboard.org/media/pdf/2018-total-group-sat-suite-assessments-annual-report.pdf on November 4, 2024.

College Board. (2023, October 4). *Official digital SAT prep on Khan Academy overview* [Blog post]. Accessed at https://blog.collegeboard.org/college-board-khan-academy-for-better-sat-prep on November 4, 2024.

Colorado Academic Standards. (2019a). *Colorado academic standards online: Mathematics—Third grade*. Accessed at www.cde.state.co.us/apps/standards/4,5,0 on March 13, 2025.

Colorado Academic Standards. (2019b). *Colorado academic standards online: Reading, writing and communicating—Fourth grade*. Accessed at www.cde.state.co.us/apps/standards/6,6,0 on March 13, 2025.

Dahl, R. (1964). *Charlie and the chocolate factory* (J. Schindelman, Illus.). Junior Deluxe Editions.

DePascale, C., & Gong, B. (2020). Comparability of individual students' scores on the "same test." In A. I. Berman, E. H. Haertel, & J. W. Pellegrino (Eds.), *Comparability of large-scale educational assessments: Issues and recommendations* (pp. 25–48). National Academy of Education.

DuFour, R., DuFour, R., Eaker, R., & Many, T. W. (2010). *Learning by doing: A handbook for Professional Learning Communities at Work* (2nd ed.). Solution Tree Press.

DuFour, R., DuFour, R., Eaker, R., Many, T. W., & Mattos, M. (2016). *Learning by doing: A handbook for Professional Learning Communities at Work* (3rd ed.). Solution Tree Press.

DuFour, R., DuFour, R., Eaker, R., Many, T. W., Mattos, M., & Muhammad, A. (2024). *Learning by doing: A handbook for Professional Learning Communities at Work* (4th ed.). Solution Tree Press.

DuFour, R., & Marzano, R. J. (2011). *Leaders of learning: How district, school, and classroom leaders improve student achievement*. Solution Tree Press.

Fleming, V., & Vidor, K. (Directors). (1939). *The wizard of oz* [Film]. Metro-Goldwyn-Mayer.

Graham, S., Kiuhara, S. A., & MacKay, M. (2020). The effects of writing on learning in science, social studies, and mathematics: A meta-analysis. *Review of Educational Research, 90*(2), 179–226.

Graham, S., & Perin, D. (2007). *Writing next: Effective strategies to improve writing of adolescents in middle and high schools—A report to Carnegie Corporation of New York*. Alliance for Excellent Education. Accessed at https://media.carnegie.org/filer_public/3c/f5/3cf58727-34f4-4140-a014-723a00ac56f7/ccny_report_2007_writing.pdf on March 13, 2025.

Haladyna, T. M. (2016). Item analysis for selected-response test items. In S. Lane, M. R. Raymond, & T. M. Haladyna (Eds.), *Handbook of test development* (2nd ed., pp. 392–409). Taylor & Francis.

Haladyna, T. M., & Downing, S. M. (2004). Construct-irrelevant variance in high-stakes testing. *Educational Measurement: Issues and Practice, 23*(1), 17–27.

Higham, P. A., Zengel, B., Bartlett, L. K., & Hadwin, J. A. (2022). The benefits of successive relearning on multiple learning outcomes. *Journal of Educational Psychology, 114*(5), 928–944.

Kelly, F. J. (1914). *Teachers' marks: Their variability and standardization.* Teachers College Press.

Kelly, F. J. (1916). The Kansas Silent Reading Tests. *Journal of Educational Psychology, 7*(2), 63–80.

Kintsch, W. (1974). *The representation of meaning in memory.* Erlbaum.

Levy, M. (2020, June 3). Cicadas are delightful weirdos you should learn to love. *Smithsonian Magazine.* Accessed at www.smithsonianmag.com/science-nature/what-are-cicadas-180975009 on May 21, 2025.

Mager, R. F. (1962). *Preparing instructional objectives.* Fearon.

Marzano, R. J. (2017). *The new art and science of teaching.* Solution Tree Press.

Marzano, R. J. (2018). *Making classroom assessments reliable and valid.* Marzano Resources.

Marzano, R. J., & Abbott, S. D. (2022). *Teaching in a competency-based elementary school: The Marzano Academies model.* Marzano Resources.

Marzano, R. J., Aschoff, A. S., & Avila, A. (2022). *Teaching in a competency-based secondary school: The Marzano Academies model.* Marzano Resources.

Marzano, R. J., Brandt, R. S., Hughes, C. S., Jones, B. F., Presseisen, B. Z., Rankin, S. C., et al. (1988). *Dimensions of thinking: A framework for curriculum and instruction.* ASCD.

Marzano, R. J., Dodson, C. W., Simms, J. A., & Wipf, J. P. (2022). *Ethical test preparation in the classroom.* Marzano Resources.

Marzano, R. J., & Hardy, P. B. (2023). *Leading a competency-based secondary school: The Marzano Academies model.* Marzano Resources.

Marzano, R. J., & Kendall, J. S. (1996). *A comprehensive guide to designing standards-based districts, schools, and classrooms.* ASCD.

Marzano, R. J., & Kosena, B. J. (2022). *Leading a competency-based elementary school: The Marzano Academies model.* Marzano Resources.

Marzano, R. J., Norford, J. S., & Ruyle, M. (2019). *The new art and science of classroom assessment.* Marzano Resources.

Marzano, R. J., & Simms, J. A. (2014). *Questioning sequences in the classroom.* Marzano Resources.

Marzano, R. J., Warrick, P. B., & Acosta, M. I. (2024). *Five big ideas for leading a High Reliability School.* Marzano Resources.

Marzano, R. J., Warrick, P. B., Rains, C. L., & DuFour, R. (2018). *Leading a High Reliability School.* Solution Tree Press.

Marzano, R. J., Yanoski, D. C., Hoegh, J. K., & Simms, J. A. (2013). *Using Common Core standards to enhance classroom instruction and assessment.* Marzano Resources.

Messick, S. (1989). Validity. In R. L. Linn (Ed.), *Educational measurement* (3rd ed., pp. 13–103). Macmillan.

National Governors Association Center for Best Practices & Council of Chief State School Officers. (2010a). *Common Core State Standards for English language arts and literacy in history/social studies, science, and technical subjects*. Authors. Accessed at https://corestandards.org/wp-content/uploads/2023/09/ELA_Standards1.pdf on November 4, 2024.

National Governors Association Center for Best Practices & Council of Chief State School Officers. (2010b). *Common Core State Standards for mathematics*. Authors. Accessed at https://corestandards.org/wp-content/uploads/2023/09/Math_Standards1.pdf on November 4, 2024.

National Research Council. (2004). Buggy algorithms. In M. S. Donovan & J. W. Pellegrino (Eds.), *Learning and instruction: A SERP research agenda* (p. 69). National Academies Press.

NGSS Lead States. (2013). *Next Generation Science Standards: For states, by states*. National Academies Press.

Oakley, B., Rogowsky, B., & Sejnowski, T. (2021). *Uncommon sense teaching: Practical insights in brain science to help students learn*. TarcherPerigee.

OpenAI. (2023). *ChatGPT* (December 11 version) [Large language model]. Accessed at https://chat.openai.com/chat on December 11, 2023.

Peace Corps. (n.d.). *The founding moment*. Accessed at www.peacecorps.gov/about-the-agency/history/founding-moment on March 5, 2025.

Rosaroso, R. C. (2015). Using reliability measures in test validation. *European Scientific Journal, 11*(18), 369–377.

Schank, R. C., & Abelson, R. P. (1977). *Scripts, plans, goals, and understanding: An inquiry into human knowledge structures*. Erlbaum.

Shaw, A. (n.d.). *Cicada*. National Geographic Kids. Accessed at https://kids.nationalgeographic.com/animals/invertebrates/facts/cicada on May 21, 2025.

Student Achievement Partners. (2018). *Research supporting the Common Core ELA/literacy shifts and standards*. Accessed at https://achievethecore.org/page/2669/research-supporting-the-common-core-ela-literacy-shifts-and-standards on November 4, 2024.

U.S. Congress, Office of Technology Assessment. (1992, February). *Testing in American schools: Asking the right questions* (OTA-SET-519). U.S. Government Printing Office. Accessed at https://files.eric.ed.gov/fulltext/ED340770.pdf on March 14, 2025.

INDEX

#

10-2-2 model, 69

A

academic content. *See also* connecting ELA item frames to academic content; connecting mathematics item frames to academic content
    fallacies of large-scale assessments, 104–106
    and using item frames in classroom instruction, 35, 37–38, 57–59

Alpha and Beta tests, 11

Anderson, A., adaptations from the field, 95–96

artificial intelligence (AI), 80–81, 86–87

assessment-literacy campaigns, 113–114

assessments. *See also* external assessments
    fallacy 1, 104–106
    fallacy 2, 106–109
    fallacy 3, 109–112
    interpreting scores on a large-scale assessment, 112–113
    matching item frames to common assessments, 23–25, 51–52
    use of specific terms, 17

AVID (Advancement Via Individual Determination), 68–69

B

Bowen, S., 125

buggy algorithms, 83

C

chunking, 69

close-reading skills, 11. *See also* reading

collaborative teams
    common assessments and, 23–24, 51–52
    encouraging collaboration and co-teaching, 121

common assessments, 23–25, 51–52. *See also* assessments

conditions and instructional objectives, 29

confidence intervals (CIs), 107–109

connecting ELA item frames to academic content. *See also* English language arts (ELA); using ELA item frames in classroom instruction
    about, 17–20
    general findings, 18
    high-frequency item frames and, 30–32
    integrating item frames into proficiency scales, 27, 29–30
    matching item frames to common assessments, 23–25
    matching item frames to the curriculum, 22–23
    matching item frames to proficiency scales, 25–27
    matching item frames to standards, 20–22
    summary, 32

connecting mathematics item frames to academic content. *See also* mathematics; using mathematics item frames in classroom instruction
    about, 45, 47
    integrating item frames into proficiency scales, 54–56
    matching item frames to common assessments, 51–52
    matching item frames to curriculum, 49–51
    matching item frames to proficiency scales, 52–54
    matching item frames to standards, 47–49
    summary, 54–56

constructed-response items, 18, 20

construct-irrelevant variance, 8, 102–103

co-teaching, 121

criterion and instructional objectives, 29

cumulative review. *See also* supporting and integrating the use of item frames
    about, 65–66
    frequency of, 69–70

journaling and, 71–72, 74
related strategies and, 68–69
role of item frames in, 66–67
successive relearning instructional cycle and, 88–89
curriculum
matching item frames to the ELA curriculum, 22–23
matching item frames to the mathematics curriculum, 49–51

D

data/quick data, 122, 123
Davis, C., adaptations from the field, 128–129
declarative knowledge, 82, 83
DePascale, C., 102–103
detail items. *See also* item frames
directions for creating, 22
proficiency scales and, 26
sample of, 21, 27
Dodson, C., 13
domain sampling, 105–106
Downing, S., 102
DuFour, Rebecca, 23–24
DuFour, Richard, 23–24

E

Eaker, R., 23–24
elements, use of term, 105. *See also* standards
end-of-year assessments, use of term, 17. *See also* assessments
English language arts (ELA). *See also* connecting ELA item frames to academic content; using ELA item frames in classroom instruction
Colorado state standards, 20–21
general findings from ELA study, 18
guided discourse with, 84–88
proficiency scale for, 25–26
sample fourth-grade reading item, 4
topics addressed in, 19–20
types of items found on ELA tests, 33
equivalent expressions examples, 57–59, 60–61, 61–63. *See also* mathematics
errors and misconceptions
analyzing student errors, 117
and guided discourse, 80, 82–83, 84
and interpreting scores on a large-scale assessment, 112–113
standard error of measurement, 106–107, 108
Ethical Test Preparation in the Classroom (Marzano, Dodson, Simms, and Wipf), 13, 17, 20–25, 30, 45, 48–51, 124, 127
evidence
evidence chart and observation scale, 119
performance scales and, 122–123
questioning techniques and, 75–76
test-specific thinking and, 6
external assessments. *See also* assessments; large-scale assessments
limitations of, 103–112
test-specific thinking and, 3, 5–9
use of term, 17

F

fallacies of large-scale assessments. *See also* assessments; large-scale assessments
fallacy 1: assessments as measure of content in a given subject area, 104–106
fallacy 2: assessments as accurate measure of student's knowledge, 106–109
fallacy 3: student's ability to answer correctly, 109–112
families and homes, sending item frames home, 114–115
Fox, R., 125
Fritz, M., adaptations from the field, 91–93

G

Gallegos, E., adaptations from the field, 93–94
geometry, 48–49. *See also* mathematics
Gong, B., 102–103
Graham, S., 71
guided discourse. *See also* supporting and integrating the use of item frames
about, 77
successive relearning instructional cycle and, 89
with ELA items, 84–88
with mathematic items, 77–84

H

Haladyna, T., 102
Howsden, A., 125

I

instruction relevancy, 101, 102
instructional objectives, 29
introduction, revealing an inconvenient truth, 1–2
item frames. *See also* leading item-frame usage at the school and district level; supporting and integrating the use of item frames
about, 20
common assessments, matching to, 23–25, 51–52
cumulative review and, 66–67
curriculum, matching to, 22–23, 49–51

Index

ELA item frames. *See* connecting ELA item frames to academic content; using ELA item frames in classroom instruction
    item-frame initiatives, monitoring effectiveness of, 121–123
    journaling and, 72, 74
    mathematics item frames. *See* connecting mathematics item frames to academic content; using mathematics item frames in classroom instruction
    proficiency scales, integrating into, 27, 29–30, 54–56
    proficiency scales, matching to, 25–27, 52–54
    schemas and, 15
    sending item frames home, 114–115
    standards, matching to, 20–22, 47–49
item schemas, necessity of understanding, 12–15. *See also* schemas

J

journaling. *See also* supporting and integrating the use of item frames
    about, 70–71
    cumulative review and, 71–72
    finding time for, 74
    item frames and, 72
    metacognitive skills and, 72–74
    successive relearning instructional cycle and, 89

K

Kelly, F., 9, 10
Kiuhara, S., 71

L

lagging indicators, 122, 123
large-scale assessments. *See also* assessments
    fallacy 1: assessments as measure of content in a given subject area, 104–106
    fallacy 2: assessments as accurate measure of student's knowledge, 106–109
    fallacy 3: student's ability to answer correctly, 109–112
    interpretation of a student's score on, 112–113
    use of term, 17
leading indicators, 122, 123
leading item-frame usage at the school and district level. *See also* item frames
    about, 101
    adaptations from the field, 123–131
    interpretation of a student's score on a large-scale assessment, 112–113
    limitations of external tests, 103–112
    schoolwide initiatives, 113–123
    summary, 131
    teaching to the test, misconceptions about, 101–103
Lynch, D., 125
Lynch, M., adaptations from the field, 123–125

M

MacKay, M., 71
Many, T., 23–24
Martin, B., adaptations from the field, 129–131
Marzano, R., 13
mathematics. *See also* connecting mathematics item frames to academic content; using mathematics item frames in classroom instruction
    Colorado state standards, 47–48
    equivalent expressions problems, 60, 61, 62
    example fifth-grade mathematics item, 52
    example third-grade mathematics item, 7
    fallacies of large-scale assessments and, 109–112
    guided discourse with, 77–84
    proficiency scales for, 53, 54–55
    rates and ratios, 50–51, 54
    student survey of mathematics content, 59
    topics by grade level, 46–47, 70
measurement topics, 70
Messick, S., 8
metacognitive skills, 72–74
multiple choice
    rise of, 9–11
    test-specific thinking and, 5–6
Mussman, G., adaptations from the field, 96–99

O

observations
    classroom observations and teacher feedback, 117–118, 120
    evidence chart and observation scale, 119
Office of Technology Assessment, 9

P

Paris, J., 124
Pearson, L., adaptations from the field, 126–127
performance and instructional objectives, 29
performance scale, 122–123
Peterson, B., adaptations from the field, 89–91
planned questions, 89. *See also* questioning techniques
probing students' thinking, 80–82
procedural knowledge, 83

proficiency scales
　example of for ELA, 25–26
　examples of for mathematics, 53, 58
　examples of with embedded item frames, 27–29, 36–37, 54–55
　integrating item frames into, 27, 29–30, 54–56
　matching item frames to, 25–27, 52–54

Q

questioning techniques, 74–77, 89. *See also* supporting and integrating the use of item frames
quick data, 122, 123

R

rates and ratios, 50–51, 54. *See also* mathematics
reading. *See also* English language arts (ELA)
　close-reading skills, 11
　sample fourth-grade reading item, 4
　silent reading tests, 10
record phase, 66–67, 71
reflections, teacher reflection tool, 120
review phase, 66, 67, 71
revise phase, 66, 68, 72
Romero, S., 125

S

Salazar, A., 125
schemas
　item frames and, 15
　necessity of understanding item schema, 12–15
　schema picture, 14
schoolwide initiatives. *See also* leading item-frame usage at the school and district level
　about, 113
　analyzing student errors and, 117
　assessment-literacy campaigns and, 113–114
　classroom observations and teacher feedback and, 117–118, 120
　collaboration and co-teaching, encouraging, 121
　information from students and, 115–116
　information from teachers and, 120–121
　item-frame initiatives, monitoring effectiveness of, 121–123
　sending item frames home, 114–115
selected-response items, 18, 19, 30, 31
Shelofsky, D., 125
silent reading tests, 10. *See also* reading
Simms, J., 13
standard error of measurement (SEM), 106–107, 108

standards
　domain sampling and, 105–106
　large-scale assessment fallacies and, 104–106
　matching item frames to, 20–22, 47–49
state assessments, use of term, 17. *See also* external assessments
student alterations and using item frames in classroom instruction, 41–42, 62
student-generated items and using item frames in classroom instruction, 42–43, 63
subject-verb agreement, 23
successive relearning
　instructional cycle, 88–89. *See also* supporting and integrating the use of item frames
　use of term, 65
supporting and integrating the use of item frames. *See also* item frames
　about, 65
　adaptations from the field, 89–99
　cumulative review, 65–70
　guided discourse, 77–88
　journaling, 70–74
　questioning techniques, 74–77
　successive relearning instructional cycle, 88–89
　summary, 99
surveys
　examples of student surveys, 38, 59
　obtaining information from students, 115–116

T

teacher alterations and using item frames in classroom instruction, 39–41, 61–62
teacher reflection tool, 120
teaching to the test
　misconceptions about, 101–103
　and sending item frames home, 114
test familiarization, 101, 102
test preparation, use of term, 101
test-specific thinking
　about, 2, 3
　defense of, 11–12
　necessity of understanding item schema and, 12–15
　rise of multiple choice and, 9–11
　summary, 15
　test-specific thinking and external assessments, 3, 5–9
test-taking tricks, 102
Tidd, C., adaptations from the field, 94–95
Trujillo, C., adaptations from the field, 127–128

Index

U

understanding test-specific thinking. *See* test-specific thinking

using ELA item frames in classroom instruction. *See also* English language arts (ELA); item frames
- about, 35
- step 1: teaching the content that is the focus of the item frame, 35, 37–38
- step 2: presenting students with potential strategies for approaching the item, 38–39
- step 3: providing students with multiple opportunities to analyze items, 39–43
- summary, 44

using mathematics item frames in classroom instruction. *See also* item frames; mathematics
- about, 57
- step 1: teaching the content that is the focus of the item frame, 57–59
- step 2: presenting students with potential strategies for approaching the item, 60–61
- step 3: providing students with multiple opportunities to analyze items, 61–63
- summary, 63

W

Wipf, J., 13

writing to learn, use of term, 71. *See also* journaling

Ethical Test Preparation in the Classroom
Robert J. Marzano, Christopher W. Dodson, Julia A. Simms, and Jacob P. Wipf
Large-scale assessments—and the conclusions drawn from them—have the power to either open or close future doors for your students. Based on the latest research, this resource clearly articulates everything you need to know about ethical and effective test preparation.
BKL059

The New Art and Science of Classroom Assessment
Robert J. Marzano, Jennifer S. Norford, and Mike Ruyle
Shift to a new paradigm of classroom assessment that is more meaningful and accurate. Step by step, the authors outline a clear path for transitioning to a holistic mode of assessment that truly reflects course curriculum and student progress.
BKF788

Where Learning Happens
Julia A. Simms
Explore the types of attention—sustained, selective, divided, and effective—in depth and gain research-suggested strategies to maximize student attention and engagement. By understanding cognitive load theory, information-processing principles, and other key concepts, teachers can leverage attention-related strategies to help students achieve their academic goals.
BKL078

Assessing Learning in the Standards-Based Classroom
Jan K. Hoegh, Jeff Flygare, Tammy Heflebower, and Philip B. Warrick
Successful assessments provide meaningful data that inform your next instructional steps. With the help of this practical guide, learn how to successfully integrate assessment with the standards-based teaching and learning process to improve student performance and evaluate instructional efficacy.
BKL070

Visit MarzanoResources.com or call 888.849.0851 to order.

Professional Development Designed for Success

Empower your staff to tap into their full potential as educators. As an all-inclusive research-into-practice resource center, we are committed to helping your school or district become highly effective at preparing every student for his or her future.

Choose from our wide range of customized professional development opportunities for teachers, administrators, and district leaders. Each session offers hands-on support, personalized answers, and accessible strategies that can be put into practice immediately.

Bring Marzano Resources experts to your school for results-oriented training on:

- Assessment & Grading
- Curriculum
- Instruction
- School Leadership
- Teacher Effectiveness
- Student Engagement
- Vocabulary
- Competency-Based Education

LEARN MORE at MarzanoResources.com/PD